BARBARA STANWYCK

BARBARA STANWYCK

A Pyramid Illustrated History of the Movies

by
Jerry Vermilye

General Editor: **TED SENNETT**

PUBLICATIONS
NEW YORK

*For
Natalie—
whose taste is impeccable*

**BARBARA STANWYCK
A Pyramid Illustrated History of the Movies**

Copyright © 1975 by Pyramid Communications, Inc.

All rights reserved. No part of this book may be reproduced in any form or by any electronic or mechanical means including information storage and retrieval systems without permission in writing from the Publisher, except by a reviewer who may quote brief passages in a review.

Pyramid edition published February 1975

ISBN 0-515-03641-2
Library of Congress Catalog Card Number: 74-24838

Printed in the United States of America

Pyramid Books are published by Pyramid Communications, Inc. Its trademarks, consisting of the word "Pyramid" and the portrayal of a pyramid, are registered in the United States Patent Office.

Pyramid Communications, Inc., 919 Third Avenue, New York, N.Y. 10022

CONDITIONS OF SALE

"Any sale, lease, transfer or circulation of this book by way of trade or in quantities of more than one copy, without the original cover bound thereon, will be construed by the Publisher as evidence that the parties to such transaction have illegal possession of the book, and will subject them to claim by the Publisher and prosecution under the law."

(graphic design by anthony basile)

ACKNOWLEDGMENTS

Alfred Boone, George Caudill, Kenneth G. Lawrence's Movie Memorabilia Shop of Hollywood, Leonard Maltin, Doug McClelland, Mark Ricci's Memory Shop, Metromedia Television (Mike Stephens), The Museum of Modern Art (Charles Silver), James Robert Parish, Romano Tozzi, and United Artists/16 (Donald Krim).

And the companies that made and distributed Barbara Stanwyck's films: The American Broadcasting Co., Columbia Pictures, First National Pictures, Metro-Goldwyn-Mayer, Inc., Paramount Pictures Corp., Republic Pictures, RKO Radio Pictures, 20th Century-Fox Film Corp., United Artists, Universal Pictures and Warner Bros. Inc.

CONTENTS

Introduction	11
Stevens to Stanwyck: Up from Brooklyn	14
Hollywood: The Depression Heroine	21
Recognition by Oscar: Always a Bridesmaid	58
Light Comedy/Dark Drama	78
The Middle Years: Suds and Programmers	102
The Queen: Drawing Room to Sagebrush	116
The Grand Dame: Television and a New Career	129
Bibliography	141
The Films of Barbara Stanwyck	143
Index	153

INTRODUCTION

In 1970, when the Blackglama fur people released the latest in a series of celebrity ads for their product, the public saw a defiant little lady, hands placed emphatically on her hips, white hair belying the smoothness of her skin, lips curled back on a face whose fighting façade appeared to be scolding her photographer. Unlike similar ads by this company, glorifying the mature years of such "living legends" as Joan Crawford, Marlene Dietrich, Bette Davis and Rita Hayworth with flattering, soft-focus still photography, this photo captured the essence of another such legend—Barbara Stanwyck.

A star since the advent of talking pictures, she remains among the last of a dying breed of great movie stars, although it is a role that she's usually chosen to eschew in public. Not given to talk much about her private life or write her memoirs, Stanwyck—or "Missy," as she is known to her friends, fellow players and film crews—just keeps on acting—when and if she can get the work—in a film world greatly changed from the environment in which she learned her craft during the 1930s.

Like Joan Crawford, she has endured because of a willingness to change with the times, which has altered her screen image from tough Depression heroine to clotheshorse to quick-witted comedienne to murderess to reformed bad girl to naïve wife to the middle-aged lady with a past behind her and a gun never far away. Capable of being equally persuasive as a grand dame or a "broad," Stanwyck's unwillingness to retire when times were rough and good roles were few (or nonexistent) has brought her criticism, as well as lucrative work in melodramas and Westerns (a genre she loves), more recently on television.

Among the least-mimicked of the Hollywood veterans, Stanwyck is best known for her well-modulated alto voice, whose tones have deepened through the years, with her dialogue often spoken through the clenched teeth of a mouth ever reluctant to close. Occasionally, the Hollywood refinements of her original Brooklyn speech patterns refuse to give in to the demands of a low-bred character, and Stanwyck will allow one of her ladies to utter an unlikely "neeuoo" or "Tchoosday," which might be at odds with the story's background. And many a Stanwyck screenplay allows her to cut loose with a verbal tirade that strikes like lightning—and with just as electrifying an effect.

Her posture is exemplary; Stanwyck claims it was developed by long hours spent studying lions, ti-

gers and panthers at the zoo, and emulating them. Although most of her characterizations have been strong, if not dominating, she is equally capable of projecting introverted restraint (*My Reputation*). Like most of the great stars, within the varying demands of her roles, Stanwyck is always Stanwyck. "Realism, being yourself," she has said, "these are the things the big stars were made of in the early days of Hollywood. It's like that great Billy Wilder line in *Sunset Boulevard* when Gloria Swanson said: 'In my day, we had faces.'"

Like many older stars, Barbara Stanwyck appears unconcerned with dwelling on her past history. In 1965, she told interviewer Ezra Goodman, "I can't avoid my old movies on TV. Occasionally, I do see them. Well, some of them; not the too-old ones. *Double Indemnity* was not bad. It still holds up. But the real old ones I won't look at. Anyway, those go on at two or three A.M., so I'm pretty safe."

Her consideration for others who work on her films has often resulted in her own discomfort—but without complaint. Even her methods of script memorization hinge on her thoughtfulness: "I've always had to learn the entire script before I started. That goes for pictures or television. And that's the stage training. I must learn the whole thing—exactly as I would a stage play. Then I don't care where the director goes, because I know everything—and I'm adjustable for him."

Almost everyone who has ever worked with Barbara Stanwyck has stories of her kindness and consideration—and high praise for her professionalism, her generosity to others, and her sense of humor. Impatient with phonies, she has also avoided any false accoutrements contingent with many other actresses of her stature, from padding her modest bust to dyeing her once-prematurely gray hair to lying about her age ("How silly. Everybody has to grow old.")

At an age (sixty-seven) when there are few job offers that she can even consider, Barbara Stanwyck claims she takes each day as it comes, and concludes, "I'd love to make another film if it was a good, gutsy role."

STEVENS TO STANWYCK: UP FROM BROOKLYN

Barbara Stanwyck has described her childhood as "completely awful." Born in Brooklyn, the fifth and last child of a poor Scots-Irish couple, Byron and Catherine McGee Stevens, she arrived on July 16, 1907, and was named Ruby. When she was two, her ailing mother died when, according to reports, a drunk accidentally pushed her off a streetcar, causing a fatal blow to the head. Unable to cope with his grief, poverty and the care of five children, Stevens, a laborer, deserted his family and went to sea. It was later revealed that he died two years later and was buried at sea.

Orphaned at four, Ruby Stevens spent her early years in foster homes, boarded out with her slightly older brother Byron. At other times, they were looked after by their older sister Mildred, whose career as a showgirl often took her out-of-town on the road. "In eleven years, I lived in fourteen different homes," Stanwyck once said, adding, "My clearest memory is of the crowds, of spent old women bent over hot tubs and babies crying and men reeling drunk to their homes. Half the time I slept on a mattress on the kitchen floor."

Whenever she could scrounge the money, little Ruby sought refuge in the movies, where Pearl White was her heroine, and today Stanwyck says, "I guess that planted the seed." She learned dancing from a beau of her sister's, James "Buck" Mack, who was half of the vaudeville team called Miller and Mack. Her schooling was as itinerant as her home address. "I think I went to every public school in Brooklyn, I was shifted about and changed so often," she has said. But at thirteen, she was graduated from Erasmus Hall High School, and that was the end of her formal education. Economic circumstances decreed that she go to work.

Adding three years to her age, Ruby found employment wrapping bundles in the basement of the Abraham & Straus department store in Brooklyn, then worked for the telephone company and, later, in the pattern department of *Vogue* magazine—from which she was fired when it developed that she knew absolutely nothing about patterns. Next there was a job as a file clerk. During this period, she had been taking dancing lessons and, at fifteen, a want ad for the Remick Music Publishing Company led to her first job in show business—as a chorus girl at a popular Times Square nightclub called the Strand Roof.

In stroller, with brother Byron

In Broadway Play THE NOOSE (1926). With Rex Cherryman

With illusions of becoming another Isadora Duncan, Ruby Stevens had dressed and made herself up to convince the Roof's stage manager Earl Lindsay that she was eighteen. Whether or not he was taken in by her getup, Lindsay was sufficiently impressed by the girl's dancing to hire her at $35 a week. Under his tutelage Ruby worked hard and compensated for her lack of experience by learning Lindsay's dance routines quickly. Subsequently he was instrumental in finding employment for her in other clubs and Broadway revues with which he was associated. In the 1922 *Ziegfeld Follies*, dressed in an abbreviated costume, Ruby Stevens rode an elephant. After that, she danced in the chorus of the Shubert revue, *A Night in Venice*, and went into *Keep Kool*, staged by Earl Lindsay in May, 1924. One of seventeen "Keep Kool Cuties," described by *Variety* as "the hoofiest chorus seen in ages," sixteen-year-old Ruby Stevens also had a part in a comedy sketch. That August, when *Keep Kool* folded, she toured with the *Ziegfeld Follies*, appearing in two production numbers and a remounting of the satirical sketch from *Keep Kool*. After which she was one of the Ladies of the Ensemble in a 1925 Shubert revue entitled *Gay Paree*, starring Chic Sale and Winnie Lightner.

By this time, Ruby was sharing a cold-water flat ("We had to; it was the only way we could eat") with fellow chorines Mae Clarke (destined for movie stardom herself—and Jimmy Cagney's grapefruit) and Wanda Mansfield, who later wed songwriter Walter Donaldson ("My Blue Heaven," "Carolina in the Morning"). Early in 1926 Mae and Ruby moonlighted by hoofing at the Everglades Café, which, coupled with their work in *Gay Paree*, kept them exhausted but solvent. And then, inevitably, came a period of unemployment. Barbara Stanwyck attributes their survival during these lean times to the largesse of restaurateur Billy LaHiff, whose popular 48th Street establishment, The Tavern, helped feed many an out-of-work Broadway performer, and whose niece was aspiring dancer-actress Nancy Carroll. It was through LaHiff that Ruby Stevens got her first break; he knew that director-playwright Willard Mack was casting chorus girls for his play, *The Noose*. Once hired, she induced Mack to engage her two roommates as well.

The Noose did so poorly in its Pittsburgh tryout that Mack rewrote it extensively, expanding Ruby's small cabaret-girl part into the female lead. As such, she now had a key dramatic scene to carry—one that would sorely challenge the talents of a chorine whose prior experience did not encompass heavy drama. The actress credits Willard Mack's clever coaching tactics with enabling her to "get by." She reports that he met her uncharacteristic display of rehearsal temperament with the challenge that she would *always* be a chorus girl, and to hell with her. Her Irish up, Stanwyck later reported: "It worked. I yelled back that I *could* act, *would* act, was not a chorus girl—was Bernhardt, Fiske and all the Booths and Barrymores rolled into one."

Mack not only got an acting performance out of Ruby Stevens, the orphaned hoofer from Brooklyn, he also rejected that name as unsuitable for a budding dramatic actress.

In Broadway play BURLESQUE (1928). With Hal Skelly

The most popular story centering on the selection of the name "Barbara Stanwyck" to replace "Ruby Stevens" has it that Mack was inspired by an old theater poster in the Belasco Theater that advertised "Jane Stanwyck in *Barbara Frietchie*." (One can speculate how well she might have done had he made it "Jane Frietchie" instead). And so, when *The Noose* reached Broadway audiences on the night of October 20, 1926, Ruby Stevens, now transformed into Barbara Stanwyck, accepted the first critical acclaim for her acting. *The New York Telegram*'s critic wrote: "There is an uncommonly fine performance by Barbara Stanwyck, who not only does the Charleston steps of a dance-hall girl gracefully, but knows how to act, a feature which somehow, with her comely looks, seems kind of superfluous."

The Noose played 197 performances at Broadway's Hudson Theater, during which time Stanwyck credits Willard Mack with interrupting time out of his own busy schedule to help her develop as an actress by studying the manuscripts of other plays and working on them.

During her engagement in *The Noose*, Stanwyck fell in love with her leading man, Rex Cherryman. She also made her first screen test—for producer Robert Kane. An agent took her to the old Cosmopolitan studio at Second Avenue and 125th Street, where she found herself doubly handicapped, first by an amorous cameraman whose advances she spurned, and then by being required to perform a scene calling for tears—and in a studio atmosphere not conducive to concentration.

The film for which she was testing, *Broadway Nights*, was a backstage romantic drama, directed by Joseph C. Boyle, about the career and marital problems of a show-business couple. Had Stanwyck's test been better photographed and produced under more encouraging circumstances, she might have played the wife. Instead, the female lead went to Lois Wilson, cast opposite Sam Hardy, and Barbara played a supporting role as the chorine girlfriend of a musical-comedy producer (Louis John Bartels). *Broadway Nights* also marked the motion-picture debut, in a brief bit, of another New York actress soon to be an important theatrical name—Sylvia Sidney.

Released by First National in the spring of 1927, *Broadway Nights* was Stanwyck's only silent film, and one which she has repudiated, preferring to foster the legend that her movie career began in 1929 with *The Locked Door*.

Producer-director-playwright Arthur Hopkins, then casting for an actress to play opposite Hal Skelly in *Burlesque*, a backstage comedy-drama on which Hopkins had collaborated with George Manker Watters, recalled having been impressed by Stanwyck's sensitivity in *The Noose*. In his autobiography, Hopkins later recalled, "She seemed to have the quality I wanted, a sort of rough poignancy." She was signed for the part of Bonny Johnson, whose husband and burlesque partner, Skid, moves on up to the Broadway big time through his wife's efforts. But he takes to the bottle, their marriage founders and then is saved when Bonny has a change of heart and helps Skid get back on his feet.

Arthur Hopkins later gave full credit to Stanwyck and Skelly for the play's success, comparing her with the veteran actress Pauline Lord in the ease with which she could express honest emotion on the stage. His opinion was supported by *The World*'s noted critic, Alexander Woollcott, who wrote, "Miss Stanwyck's performance was touching and true, and she brought much to those little aching silences in a performance of which Mr. Hopkins knows so well the secret and the sorcery."

Among the hits of the 1927-28 season, *Burlesque* played well into the summer of 1928 and ran up a total of 372 performances. A 1946 revival starring Bert Lahr and Jean Parker did even better. This play reached the screen three times under different titles: in 1929 as *The Dance of Life*, with Hal Skelly and Nancy Carroll; in 1937 as *Swing High, Swing Low*, with Fred MacMurray and Carole Lombard; and then in 1948 as *When My Baby Smiles At Me*, with Dan Dailey and Betty Grable. One of Stanwyck's great early disappointments was not getting to film the first movie version opposite Skelly.

While Stanwyck was enjoying the success of *Burlesque*, Rex Cherryman was appearing opposite Ann Harding in another Broadway hit, *The Trial of Mary Dugan*. About this time, Oscar Levant, another cast member of *Burlesque*, introduced Stanwyck to vaudeville headliner Frank Fay, then at the peak of his career. Once earlier, having seen him on a Lynbrook, Long Island stage, where he was trying out a new vaudeville act, she had remarked to her friend Mae Clarke, "I can't stand that guy."

During the summer of 1928, illness forced Cherryman to withdraw from the *Mary Dugan* cast and sail off on a European vacation. Taken off the boat at Cherbourg, he died in the hospital at Le Havre on August 10th, aged thirty. Years later, Stanwyck told an interviewer, "I nearly died, too, getting over the loss of him."

However, when *Burlesque* closed temporarily, she joined Frank Fay in St. Louis, where he had accepted an engagement as master of ceremonies at the Missouri Theater. She was twenty; he was ten years older, with two failed marriages behind him. They were married on August 26 at 2:15 P.M., and at 5:00 the bride boarded an eastbound train that would get her to Newark, New Jersey, where *Burlesque* was set to reopen the following night! At the time, Stanwyck announced plans to retire from the stage when her play closed that winter in Chicago. A few months later, she left the *Burlesque* tour to rejoin her husband in Manhattan.

HOLLYWOOD: THE DEPRESSION HEROINE

When Frank Fay went out to Hollywood to work for Warner Bros., Stanwyck accompanied him, at that time still hopeful of re-creating her Bonny in Paramount's imminent film version of *Burlesque*. But it was the familiar Hollywood story of a great stage performance being lost to the screen because its creator's name wasn't considered important enough to sell movie tickets. And Paramount needed a vehicle for contract player Nancy Carroll.

Stanwyck then made the film that she considers her official screen debut—*The Locked Door*. The offer to play the feminine lead in this early talkie came about as a result of United Artists chief Joseph Schenck's favorable impressions of her Broadway work in *Burlesque*.

The Locked Door was a 1929 remake of an old Channing Pollock Broadway melodrama that had already provided a silent vehicle for Norma Talmadge in 1921 under its stage title, *The Sign on the Door*. The archaic plot centered on the tribulations of a secretary (Stanwyck) who marries her boss (William "Stage" Boyd, not to be confused with the film actor who later became famous as Hopalong Cassidy), but who is plagued by an unscrupulous rogue (Rod La Rocque) from her past. In a climactic confrontation between husband and blackguard, the latter is shot by Boyd, and Stanwyck is accidentally locked in with the dying man. However, before he dies, La Rocque exonerates both Stanwyck and her husband of his "murder"—by revealing that it was an accident.

George Fitzmaurice, the veteran director of such romantic silent films as *Lilac Time* and *The Son of the Sheik,* was relatively new to the microphone. Faced with a hoary screenplay, he could do little to make it succeed as a talkie, and was apparently of little help to Stanwyck, who delivered the intense, larger-than-life stage performance which was, by now, second nature to her. The movie was paced so deliberately (early mike techniques presented insurmountable problems for many directors in 1929) that even a *natural* performer like Stanwyck was hard put to give a convincing performance. The actress is not very proud of *The Locked Door;* years later she recalled, "No stench bomb ever made people walk out of a theater as fast as that picture did. It was incredibly awful. Sometimes a picture can be bad, and a player in it can be good. But I was even worse than the picture."

Meanwhile, Frank Fay scored as the master of ceremonies of *The*

THE LOCKED DOOR (1929). With William Boyd

Show of Shows, Warners' all-star musical revue. The best Barbara Stanwyck could turn up was an offer from Columbia to portray a ruthless bordertown temptress in the low-budget *Mexicali Rose*. Again, in Erle C. Kenton, she had a director who offered little help to a stage-trained actress who desperately needed to develop an appropriate technique for films. Kenton's record throughout the twenties was undistinguished, and he is perhaps now best known for *The Island of Lost Souls*, a curious 1933 horror melodrama with Charles Laughton and Bela Lugosi.

Psychologically, Stanwyck wasn't yet equipped to play a "heavy," and was miscast as the wanton Rose who, to get revenge on the man (Sam Hardy) who threw her over when he found her unfaithful to him, turns up married to his younger brother (William Janney). But, once more Rose's sluttish desires betray her, and she is ultimately murdered by the village half-wit (Arthur Rankin).

Some members of the press scoffed at Stanwyck's Brooklyn accent,

MEXICALI ROSE (1929). With Sam Hardy

LADIES OF LEISURE (1930). With George Fawcett

and found little to laud in a hands-on-hips performance that was as uncertain as the film was absurd. Stanwyck has said of *Mexicali Rose,* "I was the vulture of Mexico. I was supposed to be more of a vampire than Theda Bara had ever thought of being. I even had to entice the actor who played the comedy relief. Beyond any question of doubt, it was the worst picture ever made. The all-time low."

Both *The Locked Door* and *Mexicali Rose* opened late in 1929 to dismal reviews and attendance. Stanwyck had been making tests at various studios, but nothing came of them, and the actress reports that she had, by this time, nearly lost all the professional confidence that she had developed throughout those tough, hoofing years in New York. Domestic life with Frank Fay, who was busily filming *Bright Lights, The Matrimonial Bed* and *Under a Texas Moon,* had begun to take precedence over any hopes she had of building a movie career. They bought a large home in fashionable Brentwood Heights and adopted a son they named Dion Anthony Fay. Frank's father soon took up residence with them, and eventually so did "Buck" Mack.

And then came a studio test—a night test—with a foreign-accented young fellow who had obviously been told to shoot it fast and get rid of her. Unlike most such tests, Stanwyck reports that there was no sign of a director, script or makeup man to help her. When the young man asked if there was anything she'd like to do, she suggested a scene from *The Noose*. Half defeated by the shabby circumstances, Stanwyck nevertheless gave her best, and was amazed to find her pinch-hit "director" in tears when she finished. He not only apologized for the way she had been treated, but claimed it was a privilege to film a test "with a real actress." Stanwyck reports that the words of that man—Alexander Korda—helped her to regain belief in herself.

The verdict on the test, which was made in color for the brothers Warner, was that neither the actress nor her director "had anything to offer motion pictures." But then the test was screened by Harry Cohn, head of Columbia, which still held an option on the actress' services. And, despite the negative reception of *Mexicali Rose*, Cohn now signed her to a contract and suggested her to director Frank Capra for *Ladies of Leisure*, a romantic melodrama he was preparing to film from a 1924 play, *Ladies of the Evening*.

Stanwyck was not Capra's idea of Kay Arnold, the slightly tarnished heroine of his upcoming movie, but he agreed to interview her for the role. Their initial meeting went badly. Discouraged and withdrawn, the actress arrived without makeup and plainly attired, and acted sullen and uncooperative. When, eventually, Capra asked her to make another test for him, the director

ILLICIT (1931). With James Rennie

TEN CENTS A DANCE (1931). With Ricardo Cortez

reports that Stanwyck jumped up, snapped "Oh, hell! You don't want any *part* of me!" and ended the interview. When he learned of the ill-fated audition, Frank Fay persuaded Capra to view the three-minute Warners test from *The Noose*, explaining that his wife's negative interview was the result of her natural shyness coupled with professional doldrums.

Capra viewed that test, and he claims that it put a lump in his throat the size of an egg. He insisted that Harry Cohn sign her at once for *Ladies of Leisure*, beginning a fortunate working partnership that would encompass five films, two of which would be among the milestones of her career.

Released in the spring of 1930, *Ladies of Leisure* became Columbia's greatest box-office success to date, and attracted critical praise. "Miss Stanwyck triumphs," read the review headline in *The New York Times*, and in his notice, Mordaunt Hall lauded the film as: "a searching portrayal of a type of metropolitan girl known as a 'gold-digger'." He cited the "restrained performances of nearly all the players" and "the general lightness of handling that commends the direction of Frank Capra." Stanwyck, he added, "shows a most gratifying ability for comprehending the requirements of her role."

Blending touches of *Pygmalion* and *Camille*, *Ladies of Leisure* relates how Jerry (Ralph Graves), a wealthy young aspiring artist picks up a toughened waterfront girl named Kay (Stanwyck), because he sees in her face a quality he wants to capture on canvas. Making her his model, he also works at grooming her, in the process of which they fall in love. Their romance collapses when Jerry's parents object to having a daughter-in-law with a dubious background and his mother pleads with Kay to give him up. They are reconciled, but only after Kay has attempted suicide.

Novice screenwriter Jo Swerling, who had been churning out "poverty-row" productions for Columbia, brashly convinced Capra that he could take the director's sow-eared script and turn it into the proverbial silk purse. This Swerling proceeded to do, giving Capra a screenplay that the director considers "human, witty and poignant."

In Barbara Stanwyck, Capra discovered an actress of rare honesty and sensitivity. "Stanwyck doesn't act a scene," he has said, "she *lives* it. Her best work is the result—not of timing and rehearsing and study—but of pure feminine reaction." Capra also discovered that his new actress had a peculiar problem: her natural approach to a scene resulted in her giving everything on the first take, after which both her energy and honesty flagged. To combat this, he took to rehearsing the other actors without her, taking

NIGHT NURSE (1931). With Clark Gable, Charlotte Merriam, and Walter McGrail

THE MIRACLE WOMAN (1931). With David Manners

Stanwyck aside for a brief coaching conference before she went on camera, and then capturing her performance at its most natural and spontaneous. "She remembered every word I said," he recalls, "and she never blew a line."

As a result of Frank Capra's insight, care and sensitivity in working with Stanwyck, she turned in a performance in *Ladies of Leisure* that still holds up well. The film is now seldom shown, but it's amazingly truthful in depicting human relationships, despite the passage of time and the changes in acting styles. Yet it won no awards, nor even any nominations, and Frank Capra credits this with Columbia's very minor position, at that time, among the Hollywood studios.

Ladies of Leisure made an important star out of Barbara Stanwyck at a time when her husband's strength as a movie name was rapidly diminishing. Fay's penchant for the bottle was aggravated by the failure of his film *Bright Lights* and, after one more film, *God's Gift to Women*, Warners dropped him. Domestic discord increased with Stanwyck's success in the Capra movie and her subsequent signing of nonexclusive contracts with both Columbia and Warner Bros. .

At Warners, Stanwyck was assigned to *Illicit* and, for the first time, she received star billing.

Guided by Archie Mayo, a Warners contract director, the movie casts Stanwyck as a modern miss torn between a marriage for companionship and one for love. Free love comes in for an honest exploration and, in this pre-Production Code exercise, Harvey Thew's screenplay allows Stanwyck and James Rennie to live together in an open affair, while postponing the wedding that they fear will lead to doubts and misgivings. When they *are* married, they inevitably blame all their quarrels on making their relationship legal. Both seek solace with past sweethearts (Natalie Moorhead and Ricardo Cortez) but, through the scriptwriter's manipulations, they come to realize that they prefer each other.

Again, Stanwyck's acting won critical praise, and the Warner Bros. publicists were instructed to give her the "*Miss* Barbara Stanwyck" treatment in their ad campaign for *Illicit*—a gesture that the studio had previously accorded to only two players: George Arliss and John Barrymore, both distinguished stage actors before they turned to the movies.

Stanwyck then returned to Columbia for another Jo Swerling screenplay, initially known as *Roseland* and *Anybody's Girl* before it was retitled *Ten Cents a Dance*. This was the seventh—and last—of the films *directed* by actor Lionel Barrymore, who had guided Ruth Chatterton through one of her earliest film successes as *Madame X*, and opera star Lawrence Tibbett's movie debut in *The Rogue Song*, for which he won an Oscar nomination. Unfortunately, during *Ten Cents a Dance*, Barrymore was suffering from the crippling arthritis that was, eventually, to confine him to a wheelchair, and was taking medication that caused him to fall asleep at times during the shooting. Stanwyck speaks kindly of the afflicted actor's directorial efforts, stating, "He tried his best. As a performer, you just had to try harder." Ricardo Cortez, who played opposite her, says of the direction. "There wasn't any. It was very trying."

Stanwyck played a dance-hall hostess who knows how to handle a tough customer. "What's a guy gotta do to dance with you gals?" asks one obnoxious patron of the female lineup, to which our heroine calmly retorts, "All ya need is a ticket and some courage." This type of rejoinder, delivered with cool assurance, is characteristic of the Stanwyck of those Depression years—a girl whose veneer of sophistication never completely masks the fact that she knows how to handle men—and how to put them in their place, when necessary.

In *Ten Cents a Dance*, Stanwyck makes the mistake of marrying a weakling clerk (Monroe Owsley), whose penchant for gambling with his boss' money gets him in debt and forces Stanwyck to compromise herself to save him from prison. But this ruins their marriage, and the film ends with their divorce and her plans to marry her ex-husband's wealthy boss (Ricardo Cortez), an unlikely match, since he's spent the entire movie lusting after her—and Stanwyck doesn't love him.

Released in May 1931, *Ten Cents a Dance* made money and increased Stanwyck's following, although some critics—oddly enough—had reservations about her credibility as a taxi dancer.

Back at Warners, Stanwyck teamed for the first of five movies with director William A. Wellman, whose "Wild Bill" reputation was well earned. *Night Nurse*, their initial film together, is an offbeat picture for 1931. Essentially a melodrama (reportedly based on fact), it centers on a young nurse whose first case involves her with a dope-addicted doctor, a drunken mother, a murderous chauffeur —and a plot to kill two young children for their inheritance. Somehow, in all this grimness, director Wellman found ways to leaven Oliver H.P. Garrett's screenplay with enough audacious humor and tough action to keep the plot from getting out of hand.

The press had trouble accepting this mixture, calling it unlikely and exaggerated. Critical notice went mostly to Joan Blondell's portrayal of a wisecracking fellow nurse and Clark Gable's impressive rough-'em-up supporting work as the sadistic chauffeur, who even lets *Stanwyck* have it on the jaw in one scene. As though influenced by her past work, *Variety* said, "Miss Stanwyck plays her dance-hall type of girl on one note throughout and is shy of shading to lend her performance some color."

Back at Columbia, Stanwyck then made two films in a row with Frank Capra. The first of these, *The Miracle Woman*, is based on a 1927 play called *Bless You, Sister*, in which Alice Brady had portrayed a self-styled revivalist of the Aimee Semple McPherson persuasion. Capra fought with Harry Cohn to buy the play for Stanwyck, but Cohn balked at the idea of a movie that satirized religion. So Capra softened the satire; he also softened the "heavy" aspects of his leading lady's character. Again, a solid Jo Swerling script laid the groundwork. Stanwyck played a young woman bitter at the hypocrisy of her minister-father's congregation. Stooging for a racketeer (Sam Hardy), she embarks on a phenomenally successful career as an evangelist, whose radio sermons change the life of a blind aviator (David Manners). Eventually his love makes her repent the error of her ways. Her ruthless Svengali tries to come between them, and when he sets fire to her tabernacle, she is saved by her sightless admirer, while the villain gets killed.

With its exploration of religious fervor and duplicity, *The Miracle Woman* is an unusual and still effective film. Capra fills the movie with arresting scenes, including the heroine's evangelical sermons—she uses a cage of lions to convince her followers—and the fiery climax. Among *The Miracle Woman*'s best sequences is the intimate birthday party shared by Stanwyck, Manners and a ventriloquist's dummy, through which he attempts to express the depths of his feelings for her. It is a tender scene, and one in which both actors display great sensitivity.

Warner Bros. now agreed to pay Stanwyck $50,000 a picture based on her increased popularity at the box office and, when she asked Harry Cohn to match that figure for *Forbidden*, her next Columbia picture, he refused. She declined to report for work and Cohn took her to court. Although he won the suit, Cohn finally *did* meet Stanwyck's asking price.

Forbidden, an original Capra script with "improvements" by the reliable Jo Swerling, is, by the director's own admission, "two hours of soggy, 99.44% pure soap opera," with major credit accorded

FORBIDDEN (1932). As Lulu Smith

its three leads (Stanwyck, Adolphe Menjou and Ralph Bellamy) for what few saving graces it had.

In the early 1930s, the "confession" film was very popular with distaff audiences, and Hollywood movies were rife with unwed mothers, good girls gone wrong, and love affairs that could never culminate in marriage for the heroine. Thus *Forbidden* was very much in the *Back Street/ Possessed* mold that had done yeoman service for such actresses as Joan Crawford, Irene Dunne, Norma Shearer, and Constance Bennett.

The film spans many years in the lives of its protagonist, a librarian (Stanwyck) who has an illicit affair (and baby) with married politician Menjou. (She gives up the child to

SHOPWORN (1932). With Regis Toomey and Clara Blandick

him when he assures her that it will have a good home.) Ultimately she marries newspaperman Bellamy, who's out to uncover a scandal to discredit Menjou, now District Attorney. To save Menjou's reputation, Stanwyck shoots and kills Bellamy in a brilliantly directed and acted scene, underscored by a radio proclaiming an election victory for Menjou. Stanwyck nervously destroys evidence of their liaison and is sent to prison.

Shopworn (1932), her subsequent Columbia film, is a dull and shoddy programmer that brought little credit to anyone involved in it. Again, it's a contrived soap opera, this time centering on a small-town waitress who wins fame as an actress. Along the way she has an up-and-down romance with a young medical student (Regis Toomey) whose wealthy mother (Clara Blandick) opposes their alliance. Toomey becomes a successful surgeon and after a few more setbacks, none very interesting, Stanwyck proves her love for him is genuine.

Of considerable help in salvaging her career and self-respect was Warners' assigning her to play Edna Ferber's valiant heroine Selina Peake in a 1932 remake of *So Big*, which had helped strengthen Colleen Moore's reputation as a dramatic actress eight years earlier. Stanwyck was required to progress from girlhood to old age, as the frustrated heroine who becomes a devoted Midwest farm wife, then a noble widow who teaches school and lives only for her little boy Dirk (sentimentally nicknamed "So Big"). The lad grows to manhood and proves a sore disappointment to his mother, while, ironically, a neighboring farmer's boy, Roelf, goes on to become a great sculptor instilled with the ideals Selina always tried to impart to her own son.

Warners gave the Pulitzer Prize story an excellent production, with William Wellman to direct and a good supporting cast headed by George Brent as the grown-up Roelf, Hardie Albright and little Dickie Moore as Dirk at different stages of his life, and the studio's contract ingenue Bette Davis as an artist in love with the grown son. Selina as a child was played by young Dawn O'Day, who, five years later, would appear under the new name of Anne Shirley as Stanwyck's daughter in *Stella Dallas*.

In a sense, *So Big* is the *Stella Dallas* of the farm country, with its theme of mother love and sacrifice so dear to the hearts of an earlier generation, and Stanwyck's down-to-earth honesty makes her a natural for the leading role. The 1932 critical fraternity generally held reservations about the film itself—based largely on the episodic requirements of cramming the events of so many years into a mere 80 minutes of screen time. But William Boehnel, writing in *The New York World-Telegram*, thought Stanwyck's was "a fine and stirring performance, making of it a characterization which is direct and eloquent all the way."

For *The Purchase Price*, the last of Stanwyck's four 1932 releases,

SO BIG (1932). With Hardie Albright

THE PURCHASE PRICE (1932). With George Brent

she again worked with Wellman and, once more, she was a farm wife, though one of a very different background and nature from that of Selina Peake. Adapted by Robert Lord from an Arthur Stringer story called *The Mudlark*, this screenplay (enigmatically entitled *The Night Flower* throughout its production) cast Stanwyck as Joan Gordon, a hard-bitten Manhattan nightclub singer with a dubious past who flees from her racketeer lover Ed (Lyle Talbot) to the wheat fields of North Dakota, to become the mail-order bride of farmer Jim Gilson (George Brent, in an uncharacteristic effort at playing a Gary Cooper role). They are married at once, but there seems to be little hope of the marriage being consummated. What finally brings them together, after Ed has tracked her down and been routed during a saloon fight with Jim, is a fire that threatens to destroy their crops. Battling it side by side with blankets from the house, they overcome the flames and embrace for a fadeout that, while unlikely, signals the happy end of an unusual little film.

Again, as in *Night Nurse*, Wellman's direction emphasizes bits of comedy business that enliven the basic melodrama and help distract from the absurdities of plotting. While decidedly a minor film for Stanwyck, *The Purchase Price* shows evidence of her early development as a star personality.

Already, that self-assured, posture-perfect stride is in evidence, and already script and direction afford her at least one of those instant-hysterics scenes that few future Stanwyck vehicles ever seemed without. After Talbot has tracked her to Elk's Crossing, North Dakota, thus tipping husband Brent off to Stanwyck's past, Brent demands to know, "How many others were there beside him?" Switching without warning into a frenzy, she screams back at him: "Will you stop *torturing* me!" It is so unexpected that it's amusing.

In the film's climactic fire scene, as well as in the saloon fisticuffs episode, Stanwyck is obviously doing most of her own stunt work. As an early fan of Pearl White and Ruth Roland, she had often longed to be the kind of actress who would turn dangerous physical exploits into a career. However, the closest she has ever come to that has been a penchant for performing many of her own stunts, often risking her physical safety to avoid obvious fakery involving doubles. And there have been times when Stanwyck has insisted a studio give double pay to an indisposed stuntwoman while she herself performed the stunt!

That year (1932), Stanwyck and Frank Fay also found time to appear—along with many of Hollywood's biggest names—in a

THE BITTER TEA OF GENERAL YEN (1933). With Nils Asther and Toshia Mori

THE BITTER TEA OF GENERAL YEN (1933). With Nils Asther

two-reel short called *The Slippery Pearls*. Centering on the theft of some pearls belonging to Norma Shearer, it was one of the series made for the Masquers Club, with salaries donated to Hollywood charities.

Her next film, *The Bitter Tea of General Yen* (1933), marked the end of Stanwyck's association with Columbia, at a time when that studio listed her among their top box-office stars of 1932. Directed by Frank Capra from Edward Paramore's adaptation of an exotic novel by Grace Zaring Stone, this was an unusual story of sexual attraction between East and West. Stanwyck plays Megan Davis, an American in war-torn Shanghai who insists on accompanying her fiancé, a missionary doctor, into the war zone to rescue orphans in peril. Their car is attacked by soldiers, and she's knocked unconscious, awakening to find herself traveling inland on the private train of the powerful, Oxford-educated warlord, General Yen (Nils Asther). At his summer palace, she is kept a virtual prisoner, attended by Yen's beautiful mistress, Mah-Li (Toshia Mori), whose life Megan later saves by intervening with Yen when Mah-Li is caught betraying secrets to his enemies.

Later, admittedly attracted to the general but repelled by his (to her) barbaric methods, Megan is overwhelmed by sympathy for him when Mah-Li's ultimate betrayal causes him to lose all of his troops and his power. As she dresses in Oriental attire to please him, Megan is unaware that Yen is preparing to poison himself. As she confesses her love for him, falling on her knees to kiss his hand with tears in her eyes, he drinks the fatal cup of tea. The film ends with Megan sailing back to her people with Yen's American former adviser (Walter Connolly), who remarks to her, "I'll bet your week in China seems like a lifetime." And Megan can only gaze out across the water.

The Bitter Tea of General Yen is an offbeat film for Capra at this stage of his career, yet it frequently anticipates the exotic milieu and mysticism of his 1937 *Lost Horizon*. Nor can one ignore the obvious influence of Josef von Sternberg, whose *Shanghai Express* had appeared the year before.

In an extraordinary dream sequence, Capra underscores the latent sexual attraction Megan harbors for her attractive captor. Seated one balmy evening on the terrace outside her room, Megan dozes and fancies that an Oriental villain resembling Yen is breaking down her door with lust. As the panels splinter and the door flies open, she is confronted with a horrifying creature whose sharp, pointed ears and talonlike nails terrorize her. But then she is saved from worse-than-death by a white-clad hero whose black mask falls away to reveal a *pleasant*-looking General Yen, who takes her into his arms. As they kiss, Megan is obviously in ecstasy. And she awakens quite shaken by the implications of

LADIES THEY TALK ABOUT (1933). With Dorothy Burgess

BABY FACE (1933). With Robert Barrat (standing in background) and Nat Pendleton

her dream.

Joseph Walker's lighting and photography contribute enormously to the success of this lush melodrama. Stanwyck's often unattractive hairstyles (whether rumpled or over-marcelled) are considerably softened by his artistry, which gives Walter Wanger's fine production an air of beauty and opulence, despite the fact that we never actually see the *extent* of the magnificence that Yen's palace must surely contain.

If many of Stanwyck's fans balked at accepting the idea of her falling in love with an Oriental, at least Nils Asther exuded sufficient sex appeal as General Yen to convince even the skeptical that it was possible. For Barbara Stanwyck in 1933, *The Bitter Tea of General Yen* offered a fascinating change of pace from the working-girl soap operas in which she usually toiled so steadily. It was also the film chosen to open New York City's famed Radio City Music Hall on January 11, 1933. Frank Capra has characterized this movie as "Art with a capital A," and perhaps it was too arty for its own good, for it lost money. In Britain it was banned completely, its interracial love affair apparently ruled beyond the pale.

Now freed of all commitments to Columbia, Stanwyck settled down to an unrelieved diet of Warners program dramas and melodramas, even outdistancing her more rebellious studio colleague, Ann Dvorak.

For Stanwyck, the prison-tough *Ladies They Talk About,* with its wisecracking dames and snappy dialogue, was a long distance from Frank Capra's China. Thanks to the vitality she brought to her chip-on-the-shoulder female bank bandit, this ludicrous yarn about a bad girl and a reformer (Preston Foster), who were once children together, and whose love ultimately triumphs over her lawlessness, is as preposterously diverting as the view of a San Quentin women's division that more closely resembles a college dorm for coeds. And since Lillian Roth was cast as one of the inmates, the plot even halts, at one juncture, for a well-rendered song number—in prison! Aside from some effective character acting by such reliable players as Maude Eburne, Ruth Donnelly and Cecil Cunningham, the film is at its best when its dialogue provokes amusement, whether intentional or not. Co-directors William Keighley (dialogue scenes) and Howard Bretherton (action sequences) kept things moving, and the cast cooperated to a degree that this 67-minute film was shot in 24 days, a short schedule even for the sausage-factory methods of Warner Bros. in the early 1930s.

The studio now assigned Stanwyck to a racy rags-to-riches tale

BABY FACE (1933). As Lily Powers

that cast her as a sexy strumpet using heartless affairs with men as stepping stones to success. Although she didn't care for the story, the actress was persuaded to film *Baby Face* strictly as a vehicle for displaying a new and more glamorous image. And so Stanwyck plays the gold-digging Lily Powers in a flashy Orry-Kelly wardrobe that leans heavily to furs, jewels, bows and ruffles, topped by a collection of blonde wigs that runs the gamut of 1933 styles.

Lily is clearly a tough tramp right from the start, as we see her sullenly serving the customers in her nasty father's factory-town speakeasy and repelling the advances of a lustful politician. When her father dies, she hops a freight train to New York, where she wastes no time getting herself a bank job ("Have you had any experience?" "Plenty!"). From there it's a steady progress of men and increasingly important jobs as the film's sound track moans the "St. Louis Blues" and the camera repeatedly directs our attention upward to higher floors of the same firm. Stanwyck cleverly plays these scenes with a complex mixture of guile and wide-eyed innocence, coupled with an obvious ease at handling gullible males that is most entertaining to watch. Taking one giant stride after another, she moves from Mr. Brody (Douglass Dumbrille) to Mr. Stevens (Donald Cook), despite the fact that Stevens is engaged to bank president Carter's daughter (Margaret Lindsay). Inevitably she finally becomes Carter's mistress, well ensconced in the executive penthouse.

But the plot is loaded with twists, and now *Baby Face* takes an abrupt turn by having the jilted Stevens disrupt Lily's arrangement with Carter (Henry Kolker) by shooting both his boss and himself. "DOUBLE TRAGEDY IN LOVE NEST!" screams a headline, and Lily is called before the bank board to get a payoff that will prevent her spilling all the sordid details to a newspaper. Claiming that she'll need $15,000, Lily puts on her best underdog act: "I was a victim of circumstances. No one will ever *know* what I went through. All I want is a chance to earn an honest living."

This she gets when the bank's new president, Trenholm (George Brent) arranges to give her a job in their Paris branch, where she can start a new life. "You'll like Paris," he assures her. "It's delightful in the springtime." Glowering with frustration, she retorts, "Yeah? You think of *everything*, don't you?"

As one final plot convolution, the Gene Markey-Kathryn Scola screenplay gives us Lily's ultimate rehabilitation by Trenholm. In the end, he loses his fortune and his job—and almost loses Lily, but she reforms in time to get him to a hospital and save him after he attempts to commit suicide. At the fade-out, the bank's board members are reading a letter which tells them (and us): "He's a laborer in one of the steel mills in Pittsburgh. They're working out their happiness together." It's a sight we might have liked to see!

Directed at a lively pace by Alfred E. Green, *Baby Face* is a key film in the early Stanwyck output, because it displays her first big chance at an important bad-girl role, definitely anticipating her Phyllis Dietrichson in *Double Indemnity*. Obviously the film itself isn't worth much, but Stanwyck gives it all she's got, and her wily performance is fascinating to watch as she employs a spectrum of gold-digging tricks to get what she wants. Not only is the actress beautifully served by costume and makeup, but she's photographed with great care by James Van Trees, whose expertise goes far to convince an audience that this dame has what it takes to twist men into pretzels.

Much of the press was either shocked or dismayed by the film and by Stanwyck's characterization. *Variety* called it "blue and nothing else," while reporting, "This is reputed to be a remake on the first print, which was considered too hot."

Over the years, Stanwyck has most enjoyed playing honest and straightforward roles with which she can readily identify. She was given such a role in her next Warners film, *Ever in My Heart* (1933), a rather contrived melodrama about a German professor (Otto Kruger), who comes to the United States and marries an American (Stanwyck) in 1909. As the years pass, he becomes a devoted father, a model citizen and a popular member of the community—until World War I, when he falls a victim of prejudice. He loses his job and, finally, after the death of their baby son, to save his wife from social ostracism, he sends her back to her family and heroically returns to Germany, since "they won't let me be an American."

Later the wife is a canteen worker in France, where, by sheer Hollywood-coincidence, she finds her now-divorced husband is a spy, threatening the lives of all those in her division. Finding that she still cares too much for him to turn him in, she lets him escape. But he hides in her room, and they spend the night together—their last, for she decides that there's no other way out but to poison the wine with which they're having a last toast before they part.

The plot line may be farfetched, yet Stanwyck and Kruger, supported by an excellent cast and Archie Mayo's sensitive direction, come very close to making it all quite convincing. Bertram Milhauser, adapting a story he had co-authored with Beulah Marie Dix, gave this melancholy tale power and sincerity, as well as heavy doses of Teutonic sentiment. Amazingly, much of the sentiment works. Among the memorable scenes is the one in which the couple's little son dies. The child lies sick, and Kruger relieves an exhausted Stanwyck from her watch so that she can lie down and rest in the adjoining bedroom. As she closes her eyes, he sings softly to the boy the German melody that recurs throughout the film, "Du, du liegst mir in Herzen" ("You are ever in my

EVER IN MY HEART (1933). With Otto Kruger

heart"). But then he breaks off, and the camera lingers on Stanwyck's face as she comes to suspect what has happened. Slowly, her eyes open, she arises and moves to the connecting doorway to find Kruger weeping quietly over the dead child. With a barely suppressed outcry, she puts her hands to her face in horror. It is a heartbreaking scene, beautifully handled.

The neoclassic death scene of the two stars is particularly moving. It is dawn and Kruger knows he must leave, but Stanwyck restrains him to join her in a glass of wine. "You look pale, darling," he notes, and she responds, "It's nothing—just this terrible night." Arms crossed German style, they toast one another. She sits close to him as they drink and reminisce. He dies first, as she looks on, murmuring the words to their song. Stanwyck manages so closely to identify with the emotions of this sequence that she makes her *audience* realize what it must be like to die this way. It is a rare and affecting contrast to the star's previous films and, in light of what was happening in Germany in 1933, unusual subject matter for a Hollywood studio to tackle. Unintentionally ironic was *The New York Times* critic, who applauded the "warm and intelligent acting" of both stars, while concluding, "But the tragedy is meaningless to this new generation."

Following the completion of *Ever in My Heart*, Stanwyck financed a stage musical revue called *Tattle Tales*, assembled by Frank Fay in California, and in which they toured across the country. On June 1, 1933, the show opened at New York's Broadhurst Theater, to scant critical acclaim. In the *New York Daily News*, Burns Mantle reported that Stanwyck had little to do but introduce scenes from *Ladies of Leisure* and *The Miracle Woman*. In the segment on the latter film, he remarked that "someone has told her that forceful acting is largely a matter of hysteria and strong lungs." Frank Fay, Mantle noted, had allowed himself "to grow too flabby of flesh for the good of his art." *Tattle Tales* closed after 28 performances, at a reputed cost to Stanwyck of $125,000.

Back in California, Fay renewed his acquaintance with the bottle, and Stanwyck returned to her studio for *Gambling Lady* (1934), a melodramatic soap opera in which she's a professional poker player who marries into society (Joel McCrea), but gets mixed up in the murder of an old bookie-friend (Pat O'Brien) and a blackmailing femme fatale (Claire Dodd), before the happy ending.

Again, Archie Mayo directed her in some lively scenes with flip dialogue. "I'd like to play hearts with you sometime," remarks an enchanted Joel McCrea, soon after they've met. "I kinda figured that!" retorts Barbara in that tough-but-not-unfriendly style she had nearly patented by this time. As an acting challenge, however, *Gambling Lady* offers Stanwyck little—except for her climactic scene with Joel McCrea. Blackmailed by Claire Dodd into divorcing McCrea (it was the only way Stanwyck could help him get an alibi for his whereabouts on the night of O'Brien's murder), she faces him in the courtroom just after their divorce has been granted. He hands her her alimony check and she assures him that yes, that was all she wanted—his money. He's embittered; she's heartbroken, but

GAMBLING LADY (1934). With Joel McCrea

forced to hide it with lies. In a speech designed to convince him that she cares nothing about him anymore, Stanwyck delivers, in one take, a beautifully controlled denunciation, through which she laughs, while her moist eyes provide the only sign of her inner heartbreak. The camera holds her in close-up as she tells McCrea off, then exits quickly to the next room, where she falls against the closed door in tears. As she tears up McCrea's check and walks away, she doesn't notice his wise old father (C. Aubrey Smith) taking it all in. This, of course, leads to an exposure of Claire Dodd's duplicity—and a happy ending.

Stanwyck went next from portraying a *Gambling Lady* to being *A Lost Lady*. (Indeed, she has played in no less than nine movies containing variations of the word "lady" in their titles.) This version of Willa Cather's classic 1923 novella bore such little resemblance to her story that Miss Cather never capitulated to Hollywood again, and even left a clause in her will prohibiting future theatrical or cinematic treatment of her fiction. The critics seemed united in feeling that, without the film's title or the Cather credit-line, no one would have known the difference between it and the average Hollywood program picture.

A 1924 Warners silent version

had provided Irene Rich with a vehicle somewhat closer to Willa Cather. In 1934, as a study of the problems of a young woman (Stanwyck) married to a middle-aged lawyer (Frank Morgan), while she loves another (Ricardo Cortez), it had little to offer but a showcase for unending Orry-Kelly fashions as Stanwyck paraded them in a style befitting Joan Crawford.

Of even less significance was her subsequent role in *Concealment*, retitled *The Secret Bride* just before its release early in 1935. Here she played a governor's daughter secretly wed to the attorney general (Warren William), and implicated in a murder. *The New York Times* termed it "routine" and added that it "seeks, with only minimum success, to conceal its frailties by the violence of its pace." Obviously on an uncharacteristic austerity kick, Orry-Kelly kept Stanwyck's attire here about as drab as her coiffure. Director William Dieterle calls *The Secret Bride* "the picture I don't like to think about any more."

Maintaining a heavy filming schedule, Stanwyck then went into director Robert Florey's *The Woman in Red*, based on the Wallace Irwin novel *North Shore*, a tale of murder in the social set. She played horsewoman Shelby Barret, a girl of ordinary background, who weds blueblood Johnny Wyatt (Gene Raymond) and has to contend

A LOST LADY (1934).
As Marian Ormsby

with snobbery, slander and a loss of reputation when she's implicated in a murder smacking of adultery.

The Woman in Red is a moderately interesting society drama, well acted by a good cast that features John Eldredge, Genevieve Tobin and Phillip Reed. Stanwyck has some effective moments when she stands up to the snobbery of wealthy Long Islanders, but again the film is just one more in the long string of Stanwyck vehicles designed to become half of a double-feature bill. If, at this juncture, the actress appeared cooperative to the directors of movies she cared little for, it's undoubtedly because she was anxious to complete her Warner Bros. contract and be free. With *The Woman in Red*, she realized that goal.

Stanwyck then chose to avoid studio contracts and free-lance instead. But it was almost six months before she accepted producer Edward Small's offer to do *Red Salute* (1935), an independent production for United Artists release. This Humphrey Pearson-Manuel Seff screenplay was a curious romantic comedy, mixing the divergent worlds of screwball farce and radical politics to such an extent that André Sennwald was moved to write in *The New York Times:* "With the subtlety of a steamroller and the satirical finesse of a lynch mob, the film goes in for some of the most embarrassing chauvinism of the decade."

For Stanwyck this minor-league effort at least provided a distinct change of pace, casting her as a rebellious college girl, the daughter of a U.S. general (Purnell Pratt), who, because of her love for a campus radical (Hardie Albright, who had played her *son* three years earlier!), brings shame to her father. To separate his daughter from these embarrassing Communist influences, the general arranges to have her kidnapped and deposited in Mexico to cool off. There she gets drunk with an American private (Robert Young) who unwittingly deserts, and they flee cross-country in a stolen trailer,

THE SECRET BRIDE (1935). With Warren William

THE WOMAN IN RED (1935). With Gene Raymond

while maintaining a running political battle that inevitably turns to romance.

Sidney Lanfield, who directed many entertaining program comedies during a twenty-two-year Hollywood career, guided Young and Stanwyck through this offbeat variation on *It Happened One Night,* with what grace he could muster. Some of the dialogue is biting and trenchant—particularly Stanwyck's lines—but, for the most part, this comedy remains a weird hybrid. Perhaps the word "red" in the title intimidated some distributors: subsequent revivals and television showings have disguised it under such rechristenings as *Runaway Daughter* and *Her Enlisted Man,* and in Britain it was renamed *Arms and the Girl.*

Stanwyck's free-lancing next took her to RKO and, fortunately for her future, to a first-rate film with a director destined to be known among Hollywood's finest—George Stevens. Stevens had just finished work on an excellent adaptation of Booth Tarkington's *Alice Adams* with Katharine Hepburn, and Stanwyck was intrigued by the idea of playing America's famed nineteenth-century markswoman, *Annie Oakley*. Her first Western (a genre from which the star would derive much personal satisfaction in later years), this 1935 production cast her opposite Preston Foster and Melvyn Douglas in a colorful amalgam of humor, action and romantic period flavor, which Stevens keeps moving at a vigorous pace.

As the Ohio backwoods girl whose renown as a crack shot soon puts her in competition with the male star (Foster) of Buffalo Bill's Wild West Show, Stanwyck achieves a nice blend of shy dignity, sincerity and rural good humor. For Stevens it was another film he could be proud of, but for Stanwyck it was a milestone. "By far the best performance of her career," proclaimed the *New York World-Telegram*, while the more conservative *New York Times* qualified Stanwyck's Annie Oakley as merely "her most striking performance in a long time."

If Barbara Stanwyck's career had now emerged from the doldrums, her marriage to Frank Fay had gone from bad to worse, punctuated by bitter and violent quarrels of increasing frequency. She had tried to salvage the unsalvageable, and just before their seventh wedding anniversary, Stanwyck moved from their Brentwood home and announced plans to sue for divorce. By the end of 1935, concurrent with the release of *Annie Oakley*, she had won her divorce, as well as custody of Dion, although bitter court battles over the boy—and community property—would continue for sev-

RED SALUTE (1935). With Robert Young

ANNIE OAKLEY (1935). With Melvyn Douglas and Margaret Armstrong

eral years.

Annie Oakley's depiction of one spunky woman's competition in a man's world now brought Stanwyck an offer to film *A Message to Garcia* at 20th Century-Fox. This time, however, she had to take billing under a longer-established star, Wallace Beery. It was the first of four undistinguished pictures Stanwyck would make at Fox, alternating with a new RKO contract (based on the success of *Annie Oakley*) and several very significant free-lance efforts elsewhere.

A Message to Garcia won critical condemnation for the unconscionable audacity with which screenwriters W.P. Lipscomb and Gene Fowler reshaped history to tell this fact-based story of a U.S. soldier (John Boles) and his perilous mission in Cuba during the Spanish-American war. Some critics found the movie particularly objectionable because of the manner in which Fox implied its verity. And most chose to dismiss it as a trivial melodrama about a secret agent's escapades with spies, a comely señorita (Stanwyck) and an untrustworthy soldier of fortune (Beery) in some realistically constructed studio jungles.

Boles and Beery were well cast, but, as the daughter of a Cuban nobleman, Stanwyck was not. Some of the critics objected to her lack of a Latin accent, while others carped at her Brooklynese tones. As the *New York Post* summed it up: "There's little for Miss Stanwyck to do—but

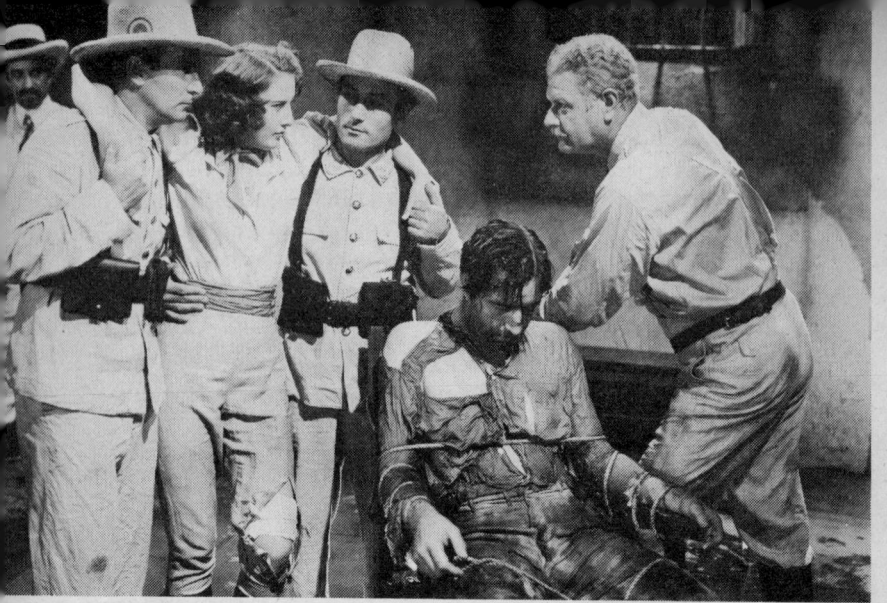

A MESSAGE TO GARCIA (1936). With John Boles (seated) and Alan Hale (right)

she has been photographed attractively and she's a good enough trouper to keep in the background when the spotlight doesn't focus on her."

Back at RKO, Stanwyck was more happily cast opposite Gene Raymond in *The Bride Walks Out* (1936), a comedy about a young couple's efforts to keep house on his $35-a-week engineer's salary. Since the wife was a $50-a-week model before marriage (hubby makes her give it all up for domesticity), her acquired tastes strain the new family budget, thus ushering in the inimitable Billy Gilbert, as collection agent for an installment furniture store. Further complications are introduced by Robert Young, as a playboy who likes his liquor, and his presence not only succeeds in making wife divorce husband, but also affords Stanwyck the opportunity for a well played drunk scene. Directed by program-comedy specialist Leigh Jason, *The Bride Walks Out* is little more than pleasant fluff that asks its audience to accept the reunion of a couple whose tastes hardly fall within the breadwinner's modest budget.

For some time, Barbara Stanwyck's name had been linked, in gossip columns and fan magazines, with that of Robert Taylor, whom she had met at the home of her close friends Zeppo and Marian Marx (Stanwyck and Marx, under the corporate name of "Mar-Wyck" bred racehorses in partnership). And Taylor's studio, MGM, not about to let an opportunity slip by, assigned Leon Gordon and John Meehan to fashion an appropriate vehicle for the couple, which they called *His Brother's Wife*. W.S. Van Dyke, whose most recent MGM films included *Rose Marie* and *San Francisco*, directed this heavily contrived triangular melodrama that was assured of pleasing the combined ranks of Stanwyck and Taylor fans. Here Stanwyck plays a model who falls for a fickle playboy-scientist (Taylor), who inexplicably rejects her to go off into MGM's lush studio jungles to—if you can believe it—seek out the cause and cure of spotted fever! His rejection prompts Stanwyck to pursue an odd revenge. First she weds his brother (John Eldredge), thus validating the film's title, then suffers an abrupt change of heart and inoculates herself with the fever virus. ("Rita! You deliberately injected that virus into your veins?") Of course, Rita nearly dies before being cured by a serum our hero has conveniently discovered.

The Plough and the Stars, Sean O'Casey's powerful drama of personal conflicts set against the Easter Rebellion of 1916, was a pet project of director John Ford, and one for which he had sought to import his entire cast from the ranks of Dublin's Abbey Theatre. Prevented from doing so by American unions, he eventually employed a phalanx of authentic Gaelic actors like Barry Fitzgerald, Una O'Connor, Denis O'Dea and Fitzgerald's brother Arthur Shields, who served as Ford's assistant and technical advisor. For his leads, the director settled for Stanwyck and Preston Fos-

THE BRIDE WALKS OUT (1936). With Wade Boteler, Ned Sparks, and Gene Raymond

HIS BROTHER'S WIFE (1936). With Robert Taylor

ter, both of Irish descent and both under contract to RKO, for whom the picture was made.

Dudley Nichols, Ford's collaborator on *The Informer*, wrote a rather free adaptation of O'Casey's play, designed to retain a part of its human drama, while expanding the action to encompass a broader canvas of a city's entanglement in a terrible conflict. On one hand, the play becomes almost a documentary of the Troubles (augmented by Ford's extensive interpolation of newsreel footage which, with its often-poor photography and stepped-up pace, is at odds with the general flow of his film); on another, it deemphasizes some of O'Casey's more colorful characters to focus on the effects of war on the married life of Jack and Nora Clitheroe. On the stage, *The Plough and the Stars* cuts through a cross section of the populace; while on film, though never quite becoming a star-vehicle (although Stanwyck receives top billing), there is no doubt that Ford and Nichols were forced to make concessions to studio demands.

Much of the movie is stirring and engrossing, and despite the obvious dedication of a fine ensemble cast, the drama is strongest when Ford's cameras pull away to reveal the painstaking authenticity of the slum houses, pubs and rooftops of a Dublin meticulously reproduced in the studio by art director Van Nest Polglase. With the intermittent bursts of gunfire underscoring scenes of bombing raids and holocaust, the film infuses its audience with an overwhelming sense of identification with its Irish rebels. Concern for the Clitheroes seems of little consequence. Nora wants to keep her husband by her side; Jack must serve in the Citizens' Army and—inevitably—sacrifice his life.

As Nora, Stanwyck employs an Irish brogue that, while not heavily applied, nevertheless gives the authentic flavor necessary to accept her presence among so many Irish-born performers. Against a slum background, however, some critics felt that she was obviously too well bred to be believed. Clad in Walter Plunkett's drab wardrobe and modest head-shawls, she makes no concession to Hollywood glamor. Yet it is unmistakably a Stanwyck performance from the start, when she plays one of her famous hysterical scenes, protesting the edict that sends her husband off to fight for the Cause.

By 1936 the Stanwyck tirades were already trademarked: the curled-back lip, the ever-displayed teeth, and the angry distortion of features no glamour-conscious star would ever permit herself to indulge in. To her credit, this has never stopped Stanwyck from unleashing all the furies at her com-

THE PLOUGH AND THE STARS (1937). As Nora Clitheroe

mand to carry out a dramatic highlight of the script. Indeed, the very fact that Stanwyck never ruined her movie-star image by indulging in these facial contortions she considered natural to the character she was playing remains as much a tribute to her art as to the affection held for her by almost every member of every film crew she ever worked on.

After Ford had completed production on *The Plough and the Stars* and gone to Hawaii, an executive producer at RKO, at the behest of a newly changed studio management, shot additional footage that made considerable changes in the film. With the idea that Jack and Nora would be more interesting to audiences if their relationship were an *unmarried* one, and the ending happy, Stanwyck was recalled for new scenes with which she, as an artist, had no sympathy. Yet there was little she could do to protest. It has been reported that, while Ford's version was seen in Ireland and England, American audiences were fed a mixture of John Ford and RKO "improvements" that would account for some oddly conflicting critical reactions—both to the film and to Barbara Stanwyck's performance. In any event, it appears to be Ford's original that is now seen on American television, whether by intent or by accident, thus giving John Ford the last laugh.

Stanwyck then returned to Fox for *Banjo on My Knee*, a comedy-drama with music about Mississippi riverboat folks. The studio rushed it into release to catch the 1936 Christmas trade, thus preceding *The Plough and the Stars* by a month.

Producer Nunnally Johnson wrote this adaptation of Harry Hamilton's folk novel about a pair of youngsters who get married but are prevented from consummating their union when the bridegroom gets in trouble with the police and has to flee. Some felt that Johnson and his director, John Cromwell, took too long getting the couple back together again, as the bulk of the story follows a good many side-paths before the expected happy ending. In the course of events, Stanwyck's dejected Pearl becomes an entertainer (dancing with Buddy Ebsen, and singing, in her own voice, both solo and in duet with Tony Martin—in the days when he was still known as "Anthony"). Joel McCrea's short-tempered Ernie never gives her a fair chance to make a go of their ill-begun marriage. Before the denouement, each has to contend with the other's suitors, culminating in a hair-pulling match between Stanwyck and sultry Katherine DeMille, who then does her best, in a river storm, to wreck a houseboat with Stanwyck, McCrea and Walter Brennan aboard. With the expert performing of these stars and character players like Helen Westley, Walter Catlett and Minna Gombell, *Banjo on My Knee* is slight but frequently diverting, though not among the major contributions of a director who was at his best with strong dramas like *Of Human Bondage* and *The Silver Cord*.

Stanwyck again teamed with Joel McCrea for her first movie at Paramount, the unpretentious *Internes Can't Take Money* (1937). Based on a Max Brand magazine story, this is actually the first Dr. Kildare picture, as well as the only one *not* filmed at MGM. It's a suspenseful crime drama in which

BANJO ON MY KNEE (1936). With Joel McCrea

Stanwyck plays a bank robber's widow who, just released from prison, is searching for her three-year-old child. Kildare (McCrea) enlists the aid of a racketeer (Lloyd Nolan) in finding the little girl, once the child's villainous captor has been properly dealt with.

Screenwriters Rian James and Theodore Reeves helped carry off this melodrama with good dialogue and a knack for injecting occasional humorous twists to lighten the tension. But the plot offers romance as well as suspense, and Stanwyck plays these scenes with McCrea as naturally as she does those of a devoted mother's desperation. Director Alfred Santell, who frequently draws on the moody atmosphere and underworld milieu of his previous picture, *Winterset*, has spoken highly of Stanwyck as an actress who needed little direction and few retakes.

The powers at 20th Century-Fox

INTERNES CAN'T TAKE MONEY (1937). With Joel McCrea

THIS IS MY AFFAIR (1937). With Robert Taylor and Victor McLaglen

now chose to exploit the continuing off-screen friendship of Barbara Stanwyck and Robert Taylor by co-starring them in a costume melodrama cannily entitled *This is My Affair* (1937). If that title shed little light on the proceedings, this well-acted yarn about G-men tracking a syndicate of bank robbers during the McKinley administration nevertheless offered authentic period atmosphere of the gaudy cabarets and underworld hangouts. Taylor played a naval officer secretly commissioned by the president to infiltrate the gang, while Stanwyck was a music-hall entertainer named Lil, whose affiliations with the criminal element are tested by her love for Taylor. At the end she saves him from execution in the nick of time by interceding with President Roosevelt after McKinley's assassination.

William A. Seiter directed this unusual mixture effortlessly, and Taylor and Stanwyck again made an attractive team, with Stanwyck particularly well-suited to her elegant period costumes.

Stella Dallas, Olive Higgins Prouty's durable 1922 novel, had been a great success in 1925 when it was brought to the screen in a silent version by producer Samuel Goldwyn, with Belle Bennett making something of a comeback in the title role. During 1936 it was a well-known fact that Goldwyn was planning to remake the work, with King Vidor assigned to direct, and was testing established actresses for the lead. (Ruth Chatterton, having triumphed in Goldwyn's *Dodsworth*, turned it down because she considered the character of Stella "too unpleasant.")

Joel McCrea was then under contract to Goldwyn, for whom he had starred in a number of successful films. During the filming of *Banjo on My Knee*, when he learned that his co-star coveted the part, he played go-between to help Stanwyck get it. McCrea insists that Vidor always wanted Stanwyck for Stella, but first he had to convince Goldwyn, who had several other possibilities in mind. Not having tested for a role since her early years in movies, Stanwyck balked at the idea, but McCrea convinced her to make the test—and she and Anne Shirley were assigned the birthday-party scene in which none of Stella's invited guests show up. "We shot the scene for a whole day with King Vidor, instead of in the customary few hours," Stanwyck

RECOGNITION BY OSCAR: ALWAYS A BRIDESMAID

has reported. "When Goldwyn saw it, he gave me the part." What Barbara Stanwyck had to overcome were that eccentric producer's preconceptions that she was (1) too young to play Stella Dallas, (2) lacked the capabilities, and (3) was too inexperienced with children.

Of course, *Stella Dallas* is a great star vehicle for an actress, but its requirements are demanding. She must first be convincing as a young woman of lowly background whose selfish desire for money and social position lose her the affections of her upper-middle-class husband. But she must also be a devoted mother to their child, *un*selfish in her desires that the girl have all the advantages possible, even at the sacrifice of Stella's own original ambitions. Finally she must swallow a bitter pill: as a young adult, Laurel has acquired the taste and breeding that can help her realize a society marriage and a rosy future, while Stella can never rise above her origins, and must be content to watch wistfully from the sidelines.

In that justly celebrated birthday-party scene, the joy and eager anticipation of mother and

STELLA DALLAS (1937). With Lillian Yarbo and Anne Shirley

daughter are gradually dampened as the clock ticks away the afternoon, and the expected guests either phone their excuses, send messages of fabricated regret, or speak volumes by their absence. We see the evidence of Stella's dedicated efforts in the fancy decorations, the party favors, the food preparations of Gladys the maid, and the pretty dress Stella has made for Laurel. The scene is carefully set up beforehand, and we in the audience know from the moment of that first note of regret, sent to Laurel by her teacher Miss Phillibrown (Ann Shoemaker), that Stella's wonderful party plans are doomed.

Stella Dallas abounds with memorable scenes, and the Harry Wagstaff Gribble-Gertrude Purcell script, while adhering closely to the narrative form of Goldwyn's silent version, gives Vidor and his cast the framework on which to hang some fine work. At nineteen, Anne Shirley (she had changed her name permanently from Dawn O'Day three years earlier when acting the part of Anne Shirley in *Anne of Green Gables*) gave a sensitive, endearing, entirely convincing account of troubled adolescence, providing a perfect balance to Stella as she wavers between betrayal of a mother who embarrasses her in

STELLA DALLAS (1937). With Alan Hale

front of her friends and an adoring daughter who is afraid of breaking her mother's heart. It is an extraordinary performance, and although it never quite led Anne Shirley into the career it promised (she retired from films eight years later), it remains wholly fresh and charming.

Charm of a more mature nature is provided by the stage actress Barbara O'Neil, brought from the New York theater by Goldwyn for her movie debut as Mrs. Morrison, the socially well-placed widow with whom the estranged Stephen Dallas falls in love, and who inadvertently becomes for Laurel the perfect mother-away-from-mother.

Perhaps the movie's most moving scene is that in which Stella goes to the Morrison mansion, finally convinced that Laurel will have a good home only if she (Stella) frees Stephen to marry Mrs. Morrison. In the drawing room, Stella confronts her would-be rival, not with anger or resentment but with resigned self-sacrifice.

In contrast to the coolly beautiful Mrs. Morrison, Stella in this sequence looks not so much overdressed as tacky. Her hair is unkempt, topped by an ugly, gauche hat, and she sports a frumpy, fur-trimmed dark coat that immediately sets her apart from the tasteful elegance of the Morrison interior. Nervous and apprehensive, she masks her true emotions with the knowledge that Laurel's very future depends on her staying with her father and his bride-to-be.

Now Stella tries to persuade Helen Morrison that Laurel's life would be much better if everyone thought she was *their* daughter. "You're the kind of mother any girl could be *proud* of," says Stella. The other woman, visibly moved, replies quietly, "I never knew anyone could be so unselfish." Stanwyck plays this scene exquisitely, her light attack on the dialogue almost in the vein of social chitchat until, as the scene peaks, she allows her voice to crack ever so slightly as she says, "In a little while, she'll forget all about me, and come to love you just as if you were her real mother."

In essence, the scene and its dialogue are more than a little maudlin, and it is a tribute to the restrained playing of Stanwyck and O'Neil that the moment, though calculated, is still genuinely affecting.

But *Stella Dallas* hasn't yet completed its attack on the emotions of its audience. Next comes the scene in which Stella, learning that the girl has gratefully rejected the idea of leaving her mother for a better life, goes out of her way to make her change her mind. She enlists the aid of drunken Ed Munn (Alan Hale), whom Laurel has always found repellent, and she carefully sets the scene for a display of ultimate uncouthness, from her overdone attire to the sleazy phonograph music. Finally, Stella succeeds in turning off the child's affections by announcing plans to go off with Munn and, have some fun: "Lolly, I've spent the best years of my life on you. A woman wants *something* else!" The girl is so repulsed that she walks out of the messy apartment—and Stella's life—forever. Suddenly Stella realizes the finality of Laurel's departure, and she covers her hands over her tear-stained, painted face. In the very restraint of this resourceful emotional attack, Stanwyck almost breaks one's heart.

The last scene of *Stella Dallas*, in which she sees her daughter's wedding from behind an iron fence outside in the rainy night, provides a final sudsy climax. It is hokey and manipulative of its audience in the extreme—yet it still works. A policeman tries to make Stella move on, but she frantically resists with, "Oh, just let me see her first —please." And, as Laurel's bridegroom lifts her veil to kiss her, Stella smiles with satisfaction. The cop forces everyone to disperse, and she walks away, her head raised proudly in a kind of triumph. It is the penultimate moment of "mother love and sacrifice."

BREAKFAST FOR TWO (1937). With Herbert Marshall

Years later, in the *Saturday Evening Post* series entitled "The Role I Liked Best," Stanwyck said of *Stella Dallas:* "There was unusual stimulation in the dual nature of the part; it was like playing two different women simultaneously. Always Stella had to be shown both in her surface commonness and in her basic fineness. Each scene was delicately constructed, often with tragedy and comedy very close." And she concludes, "I look back with affection and respect on the honest sentiment of that role."

Despite the excellence of so many of its scenes and of its performances and direction, *Stella Dallas* raises but fails to answer questions that tend to suspend belief in its more genuine moments: why is Laurel so tastefully dressed by a mother whose own wardrobe (courtesy of Goldwyn designer Omar Kiam) runs the gamut from plain tacky to outrageous? In the absence of her well-bred father, how does Laurel, surrounded by Stella's vulgar friends and uncouth habits, grow to be such a model young lady? And how is Stella herself, grown to young womanhood in a factory-worker milieu, able to manage the degree of well-mannered conduct and correct speech that so obviously charms Stephen

Dallas into a fast courtship and marriage?

In the sequence in which Stella provides the ultimate embarrassment to her daughter by sashaying amid the country-club set overdressed to the nines ("It's not a woman; it's a Christmas tree!" says one of Laurel's friends), Vidor momentarily allows Stanwyck to go overboard into parody, and she becomes merely campy and grotesque, as if her acting here were dictated by the grossness of her costume and makeup. Where Stella might have been merely gauche and pathetic, she now becomes ridiculous in the extreme, marring the totality of a superior piece of bravura acting.

Although Stanwyck has played numerous roles in which she was required to be a blonde, *Stella Dallas* marks the one occasion on which the actress bleached her hair for her art. Her reasoning: "I couldn't do anything with my hands, like running them through my hair. Furthermore, in her home Stella's hair was neglected, unkempt—and that just can't be done realistically except with one's own hair."

Stella Dallas won Barbara Stanwyck her first Academy Award nomination, although the year's Best-Actress Oscar went to Luise Rainer's affecting delineation of the Chinese peasant-wife in *The Good Earth*. Stanwyck was sorely disappointed at losing, remarking, "I really poured my blood into it!"

Stanwyck followed the demanding histrionics of *Stella Dallas* with

ALWAYS GOODBYE (1938). With Ian Hunter, Lynn Bari, Binnie Barnes, and Johnny Russell

Breakfast for Two (1937), a fluffy comedy filmed at RKO with Herbert Marshall and a top-notch cast. Alfred Santell, who had guided Stanwyck through the downbeat plot machinations of *Internes Can't Take Money*, showed an equally deft hand with the "screwball" antics of a script which cast his leading lady as a Southwestern heiress who reforms—and lands—the tippling playboy heir to a steamship line. An amusing highlight is the scene in which the two stars indulge in a wild boxing match during which Stanwyck is hit by a stack of tenpins and knocks Marshall out with loaded gloves. Stealing a large portion of the show were expert farceurs Glenda Farrell and fey Eric Blore, here cast as a butler named "Butch."

After eight years as a movie actress, Barbara Stanwyck now felt that she knew enough about her capabilities to turn down the scripts offered her by both Fox and RKO, and she spent some seven months on suspension before finally agreeing to polish off her Fox contract by filming *Always Goodbye* (1938), a remake of *Gallant Lady* (1934), with Ann Harding.

Again mother love and sacrifice occupy the actress, this time, however, on a much lower level than in *Stella Dallas*, and occasionally leavened with humorous scenes that divert its audience from the more bathetic moments. Stanwyck played that well-worn cliché, the unwed mother whose lover was killed before he could marry her. She gives her baby up for adoption, but suffers a later change of heart and attempts to get him back. Herbert Marshall, Ian Hunter and Cesar Romero were the none-too-exciting men in her life, and although they, Stanwyck and supporting ladies Lynn Bari and Binnie Barnes all garnered favorable notices, there was scant favorable press for the Kathryn Scola-Edith Skouras screenplay or Sidney Lanfield's direction of this tired theme.

Returning to RKO, Stanwyck was better served by the offbeat but exuberant blend of "screwball" farce and murder mystery entitled *The Mad Miss Manton* (1938). Here she is a madcap heiress, the leader of a group of noisy, scatterbrained debutantes who solve a double murder that has confused the cops. In doing so, Stanwyck enjoys the customary love-hate relationship with a sarcastic, antagonistic newspaper editor (Henry Fonda). Leigh Jason, who had directed Stanwyck two years before in *The Bride Walks Out*, enhanced Philip G. Epstein's bright screenplay with some inspired bits of business, though he had his hands full getting performances out of the supporting "debutantes," most of whom were new to films. But the comedy and sus-

THE MAD MISS MANTON (1938). With Henry Fonda and the debutantes

pense elements were often neatly balanced.

The actress then went to Paramount for her only appearance in a Cecil B. DeMille epic, *Union Pacific* (1939). It was a large-scale railroad drama, set in 1868 on a train moving West from St. Louis, and Stanwyck played Mollie Monahan, the spunky Irish daughter of the Union Pacific Railroad's engineer (J.M. Kerrigan) who finds adventure and romance with both a troubleshooter (Joel McCrea) and a gambler (Robert Preston)—and danger from marauding Indians enroute. Characteristic of DeMille, whose last black-and-white film this was, no expense was spared in making his Western "big" in every possible sense. Its action sequences, including spectacular train wrecks, saloon battles, and Indian sieges, and its colorful characters were what audiences had been led to expect of a DeMille picture and, in 1939, *Union Pacific* was immensely popular.

As Mollie, Stanwyck delivers a performance that is honest, engaging and full of energy. With her voice pitched higher than usual, she employs an Irish brogue a good bit thicker than the one drawn from her by John Ford for *The Plough and the Stars*. At times, her lilt becomes too heavy. She gives it a good try, but the accent occasionally gets in the way of her line-readings, with some odd results ("Is it another slap you're *askin'* for, Mr. Butler?").

In his *Autobiography*, DeMille, understandably reluctant to name his favorite among the actresses he had directed, nevertheless paid high tribute to Barbara Stanwyck: "I

UNION PACIFIC (1939).
As Mollie Monahan

would have to say that I have never worked with an actress who was more cooperative, less temperamental, and a better workman, to use my term of highest compliment, than Barbara Stanwyck . . . Barbara's name is the first that comes to mind, as one on whom a director can always count to do her work with all her heart."*

On May 14, 1939, amid production of her next Columbia film,

---

*Cecil B. DeMille, *Autobiography*, Prentice Hall, Englewood Cliffs, N.J., 1959, P. 364.

Golden Boy, Stanwyck eloped with Robert Taylor, himself then filming *Lady of the Tropics* at MGM with Hedy Lamarr. With Mrs. Zeppo Marx as her bridesmaid and "Buck" Mack as Taylor's best man, they were quietly married in San Diego, although honeymoon plans had to be postponed because of their respective filming schedules. The bridegroom's age was officially registered as twenty-eight; the lady's was discreetly lowered to thirty.

Clifford Odets' play *Golden Boy* had scored a Broadway run of 250 performances during the 1937-38 season. A Group Theatre effort, it featured Luther Adler as the prize-fighting musician-hero, Frances Farmer (on sabbatical from movie-making) as the fight-manager's girl friend, and Roman Bohnen as the boxing entrepreneur, with such up-and-coming "Method" actors (and future directors) as Lee J. Cobb, Elia Kazan, Martin Ritt and Jules (soon to be famous as "John") Garfield.

Columbia Pictures bought the screen rights and assigned its direction to Rouben Mamoulian, whose films had ranged from the harshly realistic (*Applause* and *City Streets*) to the romantic (*Queen Christina*) and the tuneful (*High, Wide and Handsome*). Stanwyck and Adolphe Menjou were set for the respective roles of mistress and fight-manager, but the difficult title role of Joe

GOLDEN BOY (1939). With William Holden, Adolphe Menjou, and Joseph Calleia

Bonaparte remained to be filled. Many actors, both established and unknown, were tested for this character that required an amalgam of sensitivity and toughness—an actor who could convince audiences that he was both a skilled violinist and a formidable contender in the boxing ring. Against the objections of Columbia chief Harry Cohn, Mamoulian picked William Holden, a Paramount bit player who had appeared briefly in *Prison Farm* and *Million Dollar Legs*. Holden was very green as an actor and had a tough uphill battle to succeed in the role. But he spent his offscreen hours working hard on his acting, his boxing and his musicianship, and he credits Stanwyck, not only with giving freely of her time and acting knowledge, but also with interceding on his behalf when it seemed that Columbia would replace him. Ultimately he came through with an amazing performance for such a novice. Years later the actor said, "I don't think there's anyone who's done more for me in my career than Barbara Stanwyck."

Since Odets was unavailable to adapt his play to the screen, Columbia engaged no less than *four* writers to do the job. In the transition, some of the drama's political harangues were either softened or eliminated, and the original tragic ending was altered, allowing Joe

Bonaparte to survive and get the girl. Naturally the boxing scenes were, by the very nature of the medium, rendered more convincing on film—and here Mamoulian turns out some of the movie's most authentic moments.

As Lorna Moon, the tough "dame from Newark" who's more than just a "girl Friday" to fight-boss Menjou (he can't marry her until his wife grants him a divorce), Stanwyck is in excellent form. Blunt and without illusions, she is clearly a woman who knows the score. When Menjou takes on the young boxer Joe Bonaparte, she agrees to use her allure to help persuade him to stay in the fight game, and not return to the violin his father wants Joe to master. When Joe falls in love with Lorna, and she with him, the lady softens, and her surface toughness gives way to a tenderness that Stanwyck's art makes wholly convincing.

In the story's climax, Joe wins the big fight, but accidentally kills his opponent. This convinces him to leave the ring for good. "I wanted to conquer myself," he tells Lorna, "but instead I smashed myself." Her response is a typical Stanwyck line, delivered with all the earthy sincerity the actress can muster: "Nothing can stop you when you do what's in your heart."

Much of *Golden Boy* now seems oversimplified and unnecessarily sentimental, particularly in Lee J. Cobb's overwrought performance as Joe's "You-a good-a boy" Italian father. But it retains solid virtues in the authentic fight scenes and in the performances of the pros: Stanwyck, Menjou and Joseph Calleia. With its downbeat Depression-era backgrounds, the film didn't go over as well as expected with 1939 audiences. But it made a star of 21-year-old William Holden, thanks to the intervention of Stanwyck, who coached the young actor patiently every night on the next day's scenes. According to reports, Holden remembers Stanwyck's kindness annually by sending her roses on the anniversary of *Golden Boy*'s starting date.

Once she and Taylor were married, Stanwyck sold her San Fernando Valley ranch, as well as her interest in the horse-breeding stable, to her partner, Zeppo Marx. The Taylors now rented a home in Beverly Hills, and "Buck" Mack, who had become great friends with Robert, came to live with them.

Paramount's *Remember the Night*, the actress' only 1940 release, although not among her best-known films, contains what many consider some of Stanwyck's finest work. Mitchell Leisen, who directed this Preston Sturges screenplay (his last before branching into direction himself), was as much at a loss to explain that title as

REMEMBER THE NIGHT (1940). With John Wray and Fred MacMurray

were the critics. It's an ingratiating comedy-drama with Stanwyck well cast as a pro shoplifter, released in the custody of an assistant DA (Fred MacMurray), while her case is still pending, so that they can visit their respective Indiana homes for Christmas. When Stanwyck's mother gives her a chilly reception, MacMurray invites her to accompany him to *his* home, where she's received with a hospitality she has never known before. They fall in love and, on the way back, he offers to let her escape. However, she has by now sufficiently reformed to want to serve her expected sentence, with the knowledge that he will be waiting for her when she's released.

Sturges' writing keeps this theme from becoming heavy-handed, while Leisen's direction and production experience helped winnow down a script that had originally been much too long in exposition and extraneous scenes to enable the film to fit the time-length requirements of the average 1940 movie. Planned for a shooting schedule of 42 days, *Remember the Night* was brought in in a mere 34 days, with a saving of over $50,000. For this achievement, Leisen credits Stanwyck: "She never blew one line through the whole picture. She set that kind of pace and everybody worked harder, trying to outdo her. She was always right at my elbow when I needed her. We never once had to wait for her to finish with the hairdresser or the makeup man."*

Blessed with a happy blend of screenplay, director and cast (including character actors like Beulah Bondi, Elizabeth Patterson and Sterling Holloway), *Remember the Night* is puzzling today by its relative obscurity. Not that it was neglected by 1940 reviewers, either. In *The New York Times*, Frank S. Nugent wrote, "It is a memorable film, in title and in quality."

Immediately after completing this film, Mitchell Leisen had hopes of working with Stanwyck on *The Night of January 16th*, for which Claudette Colbert had once been announced. Stanwyck was to have co-starred with Don Ameche in this Ayn Rand mystery melodrama, but the actor demanded script revisions, and the project was temporarily abandoned, surfacing the following year, with a different director, as a Paramount B-movie.

For a time, Stanwyck did radio work—she was a popular guest star on *Lux Radio Theatre*—and then came the opportunity to reteam with Frank Capra. This vehicle, which began under the unwieldy title of *The Life and Death of John Doe*, before being abbreviated to merely *Meet John Doe* (1941), is perhaps the most controversial of all Capra's films. With an excellent screenplay by Robert Riskin, it's a sociological—often sentimental—tale about a newspaperwoman (Stanwyck) who glorifies and exploits the "common man" (Gary Cooper), only to see him nearly destroyed by the evils of a would-be fascist dictator (Edward Arnold). Capra and Riskin had problems ending this parable, but in the final version, a disillusioned Cooper is saved at the eleventh hour from a Christmas Eve suicide jump by the love of a repentant Stanwyck, the very person who had cynically set him up as a pawn for the enemies of righteousness.

Again Stanwyck is a tough, wisecracking dame reformed by an honest man, whose naïveté and idealistic beliefs jolt her out of her opportunism and complacency. Ann Mitchell is a tailor-made role for her, and she plays it with a mixture of calculating brittleness and

---

*David Chierichetti, *Hollywood Director*, Curtis Books, New York: 1973, p. 140.

MEET JOHN DOE (1941). With Walter Brennan and Gary Cooper

energetic enthusiasm that balances perfectly with Cooper's innate, shy charm and passive bewilderment that masks an integrity unsuspected by his manipulators.

Meet John Doe was made by Capra under curious conditions that attracted much publicity. Because of its "controversial" nature, the film's screenplay was Hollywood's most carefully guarded secret of the year. First Capra picked the cast he wanted, then he approached each of them. In Stanwyck's case, all she required was Capra's assurance that her part was an "honest" one. As she puts it, "I had to take Frank Capra's word that he and Robert Riskin had a role for me that I would be proud to play. Everybody else in the cast signed under the same conditions. Nobody saw a script in advance."

Indeed, only she, Cooper, Edward Arnold and Walter Brennan ever received actual scripts; the other players were handed their dialogue scene by scene. According to Stanwyck, "*I* didn't get a script till I promised to guard every line of it with my life."

The reason for all this secrecy was Capra's concern that his and Riskin's plot and ideas might be stolen by someone else who might beat them into filming it. With the film's release, Capra had little to worry about. The notices were excellent, and the movie was popular at the box office. But the only nod it received from the Motion Picture

THE LADY EVE (1941). With Henry Fonda and Eugene Pallette

Academy was a nomination for the original story developed by Richard Connell and Robert Presnell. Was Hollywood nervous about *Meet John Doe*'s political implications?

Until now, Stanwyck had not had much of a chance to play sophisticated high comedy—not of the sort provided by Preston Sturges' *The Lady Eve* (1941), now considered one of the screen's durable comedies. Cast again opposite Henry Fonda, though far more fortuitously than in *The Mad Miss Manton*, Stanwyck plays Jean Harrington, the card-sharp daughter of an equally slippery Charles Coburn, who tangles aboard ship—and later on land amid Long Island society—with a shy but much-pursued young millionaire (Fonda) named Charles Pike (of Pike's Pale, "The Ale That Won for Yale").

At the film's start, Coburn and Stanwyck lean over their ship's rail, casing prospective victims, while he quietly sums up their philosophy: "Let us be crooked, but not common." Stanwyck wastes little time conniving to meet Fonda, luring him to her cabin on the flimsiest of pretenses. She acts flirtatious and vivacious, prodding from him the nickname "Hoppsy," by which she addresses him for the remainder of the film. In this sequence, as she throws herself at Fonda—with an eye to his millions—she's a most amusing temptress, all calculation and aggressive charm.

Stanwyck's plans go awry when a news-photo exposes her and

Coburn as con artists. Angry at being victimized, Fonda pretends to have been aware of her scheme. Hurt and humiliated, Stanwyck vows revenge.

The film's title refers to Stanwyck's amusing impersonation of a young English noblewoman, Lady Eve Sidwich, for which conspiracy the very British Eric Blore is engaged to pose as her uncle. In this guise, replete with upper-crust accent and busy ostrich fan, she crashes the Pike estate and, eventually captivates and lands her eligible bachelor. On their honeymoon train, she takes her revenge by keeping him at bay with lurid tales of her many previous lovers, until he flees from the train. Eventually, of course, they get together again for a happy ending.

Much of the Sturges humor is sly, fast and even suggestive in the subtle way foreign to the explicit 1970s. And the acting is deft, whether keeping aloft the light-as-champagne dialogue or executing the more farcical physical moments. (Fonda goes through a well-timed series of falls and faux pas.) Early in the movie, after Stanwyck and Fonda have returned from her cabin, where she has gone to simply change her shoes, she and Coburn enjoy a fast exchange of wits. "It certainly took you a long time to come back in the same outfit!" he notes. "I'm lucky to have *this* on," replies his conniving offspring, "Mr. Pike has been up the *Amazon* for a year!"

Since she was now commuting between Paramount, Columbia, RKO and Frank Capra's independent production unit at Warners, Stanwyck had no control over the release patterns of her films. Distributed to theaters before *Meet John Doe*, *The Lady Eve* scored such a hit that Columbia signed Stanwyck and Fonda for a follow-up comedy called *You Belong to Me*, and Sam Goldwyn engaged her to star again with Gary Cooper in *Ball of Fire*, both of which were released in 1941. However, before either of these two movies went into production, Stanwyck appeared for the fourth time opposite Joel McCrea, in *The Great Man's Lady*, released in the spring of 1942. It was a saga about the woman in an empire builder's life, and of how her sacrifices spurred him to a seat in Congress. William Wellman, reunited with Stanwyck for the first time since *The Purchase Price*, directed the episodic and uneven screenplay which, via flashbacks, traced the recollections of contemporary centenarian Stanwyck, from her beginnings as a Philadelphia Main Line girl, impressed by the idealistic dreams of a handsome frontiersman (McCrea), with whom she goes West as his bride. The film ranges through many eras and changes of

THE GREAT MAN'S LADY (1942). With Joel McCrea

circumstance, during which Stanwyck's character ages from 16 to 109 as she recalls her past life with surprising lucidity. Though well-raised, Hannah Sempler meets the rigors of prairie life with gutsy enthusiasm, because that's the life her man wants. Later, after he has built the frontier empire he dreamed of, and their children are dead, they drift apart and she survives by running a Sacramento boarding house. She then becomes the croupier in San Francisco's Crystal Palace, eventually winning back her husband's money and livestock from villainous gambler Brian Donlevy.

The Great Man's Lady is Stanwyck's movie all the way and she handles her complex and challenging role with authority. Years later, she told writer James Gregory (*Movie Digest*, September 1972): "I

YOU BELONG TO ME (1941). With Henry Fonda

loved that film—I was just crazy about it! It was an interesting role to play and I loved the challenge. But it was never very successful, and that kind of broke my heart. I thought it was going to be . . . but it wasn't."

In *You Belong to Me* (1941), Henry Fonda is again the wealthy but awkward young man, this time in love with a forthright woman doctor (Stanwyck). Their marriage suffers when he discovers he's in competition with her profession. Although not in the same class with its obvious forerunner, *The Lady Eve*, *You Belong to Me* boasts a bright Claude Binyon script, brisk direction by Wesley Ruggles (Stanwyck's only film with this veteran of numerous Jean Arthur and Claudette Colbert comedies), and a fine supporting cast. But it is very lightweight stuff, best remembered for the efforts of its stars.

If not for the huge success of her next film, *Ball of Fire*, Barbara Stanwyck might have received more notice for her work in *The Lady Eve*. As it was, this 1941 Sam Goldwyn comedy gave her one of her best roles in a very popular film

BALL OF FIRE (1941). With Gary Cooper

that won her a second Oscar nomination (though she lost out to Joan Fontaine for *Suspicion*, itself a probable "consolation" prize for Fontaine's not winning the previous year in *Rebecca*).

As noted in its inventive Charles Brackett-Billy Wilder screenplay, *Ball of Fire* can be described as a freewheeling variation on *Snow White and the Seven Dwarfs*, with its whimsical plot about seven professors gathered to revise an encyclopedia, and how one of the professors, Bertram Potts (Gary Cooper), gets involved with a jive-talking burlesque queen called Sugarpuss O'Shea (Stanwyck).

At her first appearance, it is clear that Sugarpuss is not exactly Snow White. She emerges clad in a glittery stripper's costume, performing (in a dubbed voice) a nightclub number entitled "Drum Boogie." In what may be her liveliest screen role, the actress displays great energy and vivacity as she charms the professorial household—and especially the ultrasober, pedantic and grammar-wise Cooper.

As she calls him "Pottsy," we can't help but recall elements of the

Fonda-Stanwyck involvement in *The Lady Eve*. Indeed, *Ball of Fire* strongly resembles its predecessor in its plot line of the meek and fumbling man pursued by an amorous and predatory female.

Howard Hawks directed this fluffy fable, and although there are many who rank it with his better-known comedies, *Bringing Up Baby* and *His Girl Friday*, Hawks himself does not, possibly due to its slower, less-even pacing. In 1948, Goldwyn engaged Hawks to remake *Ball of Fire* as a Danny Kaye-Virginia Mayo vehicle, retitled *A Song is Born*. But it wasn't in the same class at all, and Hawks considers it a disaster.

Ball of Fire is still good fun, and Stanwyck's fast-talking 1940s hepcat stripper, who brings joy into the dull lives of all those tottering professors, is a bright, glamorous and amusing characterization whether juggling the faintly suggestive Brackett-Wilder dialogue or trying to cope with the intensity of her true feelings for Cooper, despite the threatening presence of her old gangster-beau (Dana Andrews). Hers is a winning performance —but one must question whether it deserved an Oscar nomination.

Of all the 1941 Best Actress nominees, Barbara Stanwyck was the only one up for a comedy performance. She faced heavyweight competition: Bette Davis in *The Little Foxes;* Greer Garson in *Blossoms in the Dust;* Olivia de Havilland in *Hold Back the Dawn*—and the winner, Joan Fontaine in *Suspicion*.

LIGHT COMEDY/ DARK DRAMA

The year 1942 was not a banner one for Barbara Stanwyck. Aside from *The Great Man's Lady*, she was also seen in the somewhat more popular Warners drama, *The Gay Sisters*, a title quite innocent of ulterior connotations in its own era. In actuality, these sisters were named "Gaylord," and their activities were anything but "gay," in *any* sense of the word.

Using a familiar device in films of the 1940s, *The Gay Sisters* begins with its leading characters as children. Fiona, Evelyn and Susanna Gaylord are well-born Fifth Avenue girls whose mother was aboard the Lusitania on the wrong night and whose father telegraphs to the audience *his* imminent demise (in World War I) by telling his eldest girl, Fiona, that she will have to be "the man of the house" in his absence. Before his departure for battle, he reminds her of the family slogan, "Never sell the land," and off he goes for good, leaving juvenile actress Mary Thomas as Fiona to mount the Gaylord staircase with a determination that can only mean she will grow up, in the following scene, to be Barbara Stanwyck. Geraldine Fitzgerald plays the adult Evelyn, and Nancy Coleman is Susanna.

From here on, *The Gay Sisters* spins a complicated web of courtroom battles over inheritances, absent husbands and unexplained children, and subplots putting two of the sisters in rivalry for a handsome young painter disconcertingly named "Gig Young," as well as *played* by Gig Young. (His name had been Byron Barr, but audiences previewing *The Gay Sisters* expressed such partiality to the new young actor that Warners decided he would henceforth answer to his screen name from this film.)

Boring flashbacks further weaken the film's already shaky structure, and detailed legal matters don't help maintain audience interest in the plight of these characters. Lenore Coffee's adaptation of the Stephen Longstreet novel never takes an easy path of exposition when a complex one might be employed, and there is little that Irving Rapper's direction can simplify or elucidate. Hence much of the film passes before we are certain that the little boy whom Stanwyck keeps as a kind of pet, is actually her own, by George Brent—a brief, bitter alliance from her past. Unconvincingly, this alliance is resumed in time for a conclusion of questionable happiness for all concerned. When their final clinch points to a sunshiny ending, audiences can only raise a skeptical eyebrow.

THE GAY SISTERS (1942). With Donald Crisp, Nancy Coleman, and Geraldine Fitzgerald

Stanwyck's role is afforded a few good moments, including a rather extraneous wine-drinking spree in which she and Nancy Coleman get drunk in the wine cellar as one last fling before they lose the family mansion. But she also has to cope with such deathless lines as: "Love is something you cut out of yourself—or it moves in and cuts you apart." And the character frequently comes across as a rough-talking dame whose uncompromising hardness tends to belie her rather aristocratic family background. Stanwyck's attire is plain, sensible and tailored, complementing her confident posture and aggressive stride.

In the latter part of 1942, Stanwyck went to Universal to participate in *Flesh and Fantasy* (released a year later), an omnibus collection of four short stories of the supernatural, which was jointly produced by actor Charles Boyer and French director Julien Duvivier, who had recently completed a similar project (*Tales of Manhattan*) at Fox. After filming was completed, Universal decided to lop off the fourth episode, pad out its footage into

FLESH AND FANTASY (1943). With Charles Boyer

feature-length and release it as a separate programmer called *Destiny*.

Stanwyck appeared opposite Boyer himself in *Flesh and Fantasy*'s third episode, about a circus aerialist whose nerve deserts him following a dream in which he sees himself falling, while a woman with unusual diamond earrings screams from the audience. On an ocean liner, the high-wire star meets the woman of his nightmare, and they fall in love. Although she's responsive to his affections, she maintains a secrecy about her identity, and he realizes something fateful is hanging over her. (He has another dream in which he sees her being arrested.) But she helps him regain his lost confidence as an artist, and although she ultimately *is* arrested—for stealing those diamond earrings—it's implied that the fates will reunite them when she has served her sentence.

For the first time in her career, Stanwyck played a role which consumed less than a third of the film. But the mysterious side of the woman's nature—her need for keeping her past hidden, as well as her true identity—gave the actress undercurrents that allowed her to bring an added dimension to the role.

In February 1943, Robert Taylor was commissioned a lieutenant (junior grade) in the U.S. Navy, and left to become a flying instructor at Great Lakes Naval Training Station, while Stanwyck filled some of her free time—and lonely hours—by serving at the Hollywood Canteen.

Her only other 1943 release, made after *Flesh and Fantasy* but released earlier, offered an acting change of pace that was undoubtedly enjoyable for Stanwyck—the burlesque queen Dixie Daisy of *Lady of Burlesque*, a Hunt Stromberg production released by United Artists. This was an adaptation of Gypsy Rose Lee's mystery novel, *The G-String Murders*, whose title was altered when Stromberg discovered that the majority of America's moviegoers wouldn't know a stripper's G-string from a musical instrument!

William A. Wellman directed this snappy James Gunn screenplay about a mad killer terrorizing the dark recesses of an old theater and, in his hands, a rather ordinary melodrama derives some color from its seamy environment and its wisecracking performers, not the least of whom are perennial "tough girls" Iris Adrian, Gloria Dickson and Marion Martin. As queen of the show (and, of course, an eventual killer's target), Stanwyck has a few song-and-dance numbers to put over, models some wild and sassy Edith Head costumes, and trades quips—and romance—in familiar backstage fashion with the chief comic, Michael O'Shea.

Barbara Stanwyck won her third Academy Award nomination for branching out in yet another

LADY OF BURLESQUE (1943). With Stephanie Bachelor and Charles Dingle

DOUBLE INDEMNITY (1944).
As Phyllis Dietrichson

direction—as the amoral, cold-blooded murderess Phyllis Dietrichson of Billy Wilder's *Double Indemnity* (1944). Filmed at Paramount in the autumn of 1943, it was a tough, uncompromising crime drama, adapted from James M. Cain's novel by director Wilder in collaboration with mystery novelist Raymond Chandler (here working on his first screenplay). Cain had derived his plot from the notorious Snyder-Gray murder case of 1927, wherein a wife and her lover conspired to murder her husband for his insurance. In the film, Stanwyck (in a shoulder-length blonde wig, to emphasize her brassy toughness) plots to rid herself of her oilman husband (Tom Powers). She connives to make a handsome insurance agent (Fred MacMurray) fall for her, arranges for a double-indemnity insurance policy for her husband, and then collaborates with MacMurray in his murder. (They make it look like a train accident). Instrumental in foiling their plan is a canny claims agent (Edward G. Robinson), plus MacMurray's eventual discovery that he's been double-crossed by a faithless Stanwyck. In a grim and violent climax, Stanwyck shoots him as he continues to approach her, daring her to fire again: "You can do better than that." But she can't, somehow. "You never loved me," he accuses her, and she replies, "I never loved anybody . . . until this moment." She drops her gunhand, and they embrace as he, off-camera, takes the gun from her hand and shoots *her*–twice. As she falls limply in his arms, he quips, in Bogart fashion, "Good-bye, baby."

That's the end of poisonous Phyllis Dietrichson, but not of the film. Told in flashback, the movie starts with a wounded MacMurray in his office, confessing the sordid story into a dictaphone for claims-man Robinson. And, after Stanwyck's demise, we again see MacMurray in the office, completing his confes-

DOUBLE INDEMNITY (1944). With Fred MacMurray

sion as Robinson walks in and calls the police. The *original* footage went on to show MacMurray in the gas chamber, but this was ruled too harrowing for 1944 audiences, and the release print stops short of this coda.

Originally Stanwyck and George Raft were Billy Wilder's choices for this pair of deadly lovers. But Raft demanded script changes that would have compromised Cain's story, and so Wilder engaged a nervous MacMurray, best known until then for light comedy. Stanwyck, too, though she liked the script, had some trepidations about accepting the role of such an out-and-out "heavy." Finally Wilder cajoled both into doing the picture by assuring *each* that the *other* was interested. The results, of course, garnered excellent notices for both players. Stanwyck, in particular, had never created a character so utterly devoid of humanity, so icy and selfish a villainess—sensual and cunning enough to sense a man's weaknesses and invade them with a subtly aimed scalpel.

The Wilder-Chandler dialogue is fast and tough, in keeping with the Cain original, and both Stanwyck and MacMurray deliver as though seasoned pros at this kind of script. "I wonder if I know what you mean," says Stanwyck, parrying with MacMurray at their first meeting. "I wonder if you wonder," he retorts. And she wastes no time laying her cards on the table: "Could I get an accident policy for him (her husband) without bothering him at all?" she mock-innocently inquires of MacMurray. And it isn't long before she has him trapped and spellbound and he's mouthing *Double Indemnity*'s leitmotif: "It's going to be you and me together, straight down the line."

Wilder says: "The whole film was deliberately underplayed, done very quietly; if you have something that's full of violence and drama, you can afford to take it easy; it's only if you have nothing that you have to 'blow it up,' to make the sparks fly."* Of Stanwyck, he reports, "She is as good an actress as I have ever worked with. We rehearsed the way I usually do. Hard. There were no retakes."**

*Charles Higham & Joel Greenberg, *The Celluloid Muse*, Henry Regnery Co., Chicago, Ill., 1969, P.248.
**Ella Smith, *Starring Miss Barbara Stanwyck*, Crown Publishers, Inc., New York, N.Y., 1974, P. 170.

Double Indemnity was highly praised by the critics, from its star turns and direction to Miklos Rozsa's fine, atmospheric score and the expert lighting and photography of John Seitz. And the public allayed Stanwyck's fears about her characterization by proving that they liked her as much as a homicidal heavy as they did in bright comedy or sentimental soap opera. However, she lost the Best Actress Oscar to Ingrid Bergman, who won for her persecuted wife in *Gaslight*.

In 1944 the U.S. Treasury Department listed Barbara Stanwyck as the nation's top woman moneymaker (over $400,000). Surprisingly, she even topped her Warner Bros. rival, the top-ranking Bette Davis.

Stanwyck's off-screen efforts at the Hollywood Canteen made her a natural for the roster of stars (playing themselves) who turned up in the Warners' 1944 film, *Hollywood Canteen*. Written by Delmer Daves, the man who had only the previous year saluted Broadway's homefront war efforts in *Stage Door Canteen*, this movie, employing virtually every star and featured player on the Warner Bros. lot during 1943 and 1944, was merely one studio's self-satisfied salute to itself. Or, as Bosley Crowther put it in *The New York Times*, "This film seems a most distasteful show of Hollywood's sense of its importance and what its people are doing for 'the boys.'" But the public liked *Hollywood Canteen,* and since its profits went to the servicemen themselves, a little movie-colony chauvinism wasn't really that reprehensible.

Despite its true-confessions title, *My Reputation* (1946) is a first-class soap opera, and one which both Stanwyck and her director, Curtis Bernhardt, list among their favorite films. Bernhardt has written, "It was fun, mostly because Barbara is a real pal, a real trouper. You can pour water over her head or pull a hot-foot on her and she takes it and laughs. The crew likes her, everybody likes her." The director also reports that it was seeing this film that made Bette Davis inform Warner Bros. that he would *have* to direct her next picture, *A Stolen Life.*

Catherine Turney's screenplay, adapted from Clare Jaynes' novel *Instruct My Sorrows,* offered Stanwyck a challenging emotional role of a type that she had not played heretofore: a repressed woman who has led a sheltered life and who, after years of happy marriage, at thirty-three is suddenly a widow with two young sons to raise. It is not the usual screen character one encounters in Stanwyck films, and it is a great tribute to her acting skill that she creates a sensitive and properly subdued portrait of a woman on the threshold of altering her life style in a manner that shocks her mother, outrages the neighborhood and humiliates her sons—though such was never her intent.

Though soft-spoken and somewhat introverted, this attractive young widow turns out to have reserves of strength she can summon in a crisis. Rescued from her meddling mother (Lucile Watson) and a near-breakdown by her best friends (Eve Arden and John Ridgely), she goes with them to a mountain lodge at Lake Tahoe. There, while out skiing, she meets a suave serviceman on leave (George Brent), whose immediate courtship of her she resists, while simultaneously desiring his attentions.

As their relationship develops, so soon after her husband's demise, ugly gossip spreads throughout the town, until her sons are humiliated by all the talk. At a New Year's Eve party attended by the gossip-mongers, she takes the proverbial bull by the horns and stuns her "friends" by boldly introducing Brent. In a confrontation with the hostess (Leona Maricle), she demands an accounting. "Why did you come here at all?" the woman asks. "Because," Stanwyck replies, "I was still coward enough to try to save my reputation." And she leaves triumphantly with Brent.

The climax comes when Stanwyck, planning to leave for New

MY REPUTATION (1946). With Lucile Watson

York with Brent before he is shipped overseas, changes her mind when her sons run away to their grandmother's house. She reconciles with them, realizing that she cannot risk losing them altogether. In the best Hollywood tradition, however, she finally gets the best of both worlds. Meeting Brent at the station to offer her explanation, she finds, happily, that he wants to come back and marry her, after his tour of duty. As his train pulls out, she walks away confidently, tears of happiness in her eyes.

Despite the sudsiness of this plot, both writer and director manage to stave off the bathos with the intelligence of their craftsmanship, and the efforts of a well-chosen cast help immeasurably. As only one of many fine scenes, Stanwyck's confrontation with her two boys, after they've run away from home, exemplifies the warm restraint of her Jessica Drummond. Faint traces of her submerged emotions begin to surface as she tries to make them realize her loneliness during the past two years, while her late husband was a dying invalid. Finally, firmly trying to suppress her feelings, she says, "Boys, I've lost Dad, and now I'm losing Major Landis. I'll probably never see him again. Try to understand." As the scene threatens to become sentimental melodrama, Stanwyck manages to bring it down to earth and make it human and very moving. The character of Jessica Drummond demands honesty—and this Stanwyck brings, with a well-bred spunkiness that easily explains this film's popularity at the box office.

After the heavy dramatics of *My Reputation*, she welcomed the lighthearted gaiety of *Christmas in Connecticut* (1945), the first of three films with English director Peter Godfrey. In this pleasantly inconsequential farce, Stanwyck brings her usual style and energy to the role of an *un*domesticated domestic-columnist who is forced to play the home-loving type (complete with borrowed Connecticut farmhouse and baby) one Christmas season for a convalescing sailor (Dennis Morgan). It's an amoral publicity stunt that, of course, backfires when they fall in love. Eventually, she's freed from her engagement to another (Reginald Gardiner), her fraud is explained—and she manages to produce a delicious holiday dinner (with the secret aid of chef S.Z. "Cuddles" Sakall).

The movie's critical reception was largely unfavorable. Some even thought the treatment of this sophisticated Lionel Houser-Adele Comandini script more than a bit cynical, and its performance unsympathetic and distasteful. Nor was everyone charmed with Stanwyck's breezy efforts at portraying a sham *hausfrau*. Indeed, *Christmas in Connecticut* is no typical Stanwyck vehicle, and it's a good twenty-five minutes before she even enters the scene. Most of the humor in her role derives from her awkwardness with the domes-

CHRISTMAS IN CONNECTICUT (1945). With Dennis Morgan and unidentified infant

THE TWO MRS. CARROLLS (1947). As Sally Carroll

tic world she's reputed to know firsthand.

Filmed after *My Reputation*, but released seven months before it, *Christmas in Connecticut*, anachronistically, provided good *summer* fare for 1945 moviegoers eager to escape the depressing realities of World War II.

In November of that year, Robert Taylor won an honorable discharge from the Navy, and returned to resume his career at MGM, as the sinister husband of an apprehensive Katharine Hepburn in the suspense melodrama, *Undercurrent*.

At Warner Bros., Stanwyck had her own threatened-wife thriller to contend with—*The Two Mrs. Carrolls*, opposite an uncomfortably mysterious Humphrey Bogart. Under Peter Godfrey's direction, this Thomas Job alteration of Martin Vale's stage vehicle for Elisabeth Bergner was an obvious suspense yarn about a moody painter (Bogart), who courts and marries a second wife (Stanwyck), then proceeds to begin slowly poisoning her in the same way he killed his *first* wife, while a prospective *third* wife (Alexis Smith) waits triumphantly in the wings. The full realization comes to wife number two when she invades her husband's locked studio and views the details of his carefully guarded painting depicting her as the "Angel of Death." Then, as the skylight's rainy reflection runs down the canvas, underscored by

Franz Waxman's music, Stanwyck registers the horror of the doomed. In the wildly melodramatic finale, Bogart crashes into her locked bedroom through a window, only to be held at momentary bay by a pistol-brandishing Stanwyck, whom he soon subdues—and nearly garrotes—with a curtain cord. But in the nick of time, Stanwyck's faithful old beau (Pat O'Moore) and the police break in and save her for the fadeout.

None of *The Two Mrs. Carrolls* can be believed for an instant, from its phony English-village atmosphere (alive with clanging church bells and stormy weather) to the uncomfortable performances of the film's stars and supporting cast (Alexis Smith's amusingly aggressive "other woman" and the obnoxiously precocious Ann Carter, as Bogart's motherless child). Obviously the brothers Warner were at a loss as to what to do with *The Two Mrs. Carrolls*—which accounts for its 1947 release, two years after its completion. In the interim, Stanwyck finished no less than four other pictures.

She was now filming almost non-stop. Back at Paramount, she tackled her last (to date) comedy, *The Bride Wore Boots* (1946). Her reasons for not continuing in comedy: she couldn't find a worthwhile script. Not that *The Bride Wore Boots* itself was worthwhile. The story had first appeared as a 24-performance Broadway failure by Harry Segall, *The Odds on Mrs. Oakley,* about a married couple who separate and proceed to share cus-

THE BRIDE WORE BOOTS (1946). With Charles D. Brown, Peggy Wood, Gregory Muradian, Natalie Wood, Richard Gaines, and Robert Cummings

THE STRANGE LOVE OF MARTHA IVERS (1946). With Van Heflin and Kirk Douglas

tody of—and profits from—a racehorse they own jointly. Dwight Mitchell Wiley's screenplay emphasized the void between a wife who adores horses and a husband (Robert Cummings) who does not, and it's one elongated battle-of-the-sexes until he brings himself to mounting an old nag and riding it to victory, thus winning back his wife—and a trophy. Diana Lynn and Patric Knowles supply the obligatory (innocent) extramarital interest for both partners, and director Irving Pichel, always more at home with drama, gimmicked up the script to keep things moving and lively. But the final results are negligible.

Remaining at Paramount, Stanwyck now returned to the ruthless-villainess genre of *Double Indemnity* in a Hal Wallis production entitled *The Strange Love of Martha Ivers* (1946). Under the direction of Lewis Milestone, who had impressed Wallis with his war film, *A Walk in the Sun*, this grim, compelling story dealt with passion and violence in a small Midwest town. The glossy melodrama centers on a vicious, dominating woman (Stanwyck in a successful invasion of Bette Davis territory), her weak, alcoholic husband (Kirk Douglas in an uncharacteristic movie debut), and the wife's childhood flame (Van Heflin), now briefly back in town.

With an interesting script by Robert Rossen that went through such early title changes as *Bleeding Heart* and *Love Lies Bleeding*, *The Strange Love of Martha Ivers* delivers an oddly fascinating study of unpleasant people whose lives become intertwined in an atmosphere heavy with greed, corruption and murder. In the film's early scenes, the Stanwyck and Douglas characters are teen-aged participants in the murder of her wealthy aunt (Judith Anderson). For years afterward they keep their crime a

THE STRANGE LOVE OF MARTHA IVERS (1946). With Van Heflin and Kirk Douglas

secret, although they think their best friend (Heflin), who left town that night, was a witness. (In reality, he is ignorant of their guilt, and it is not until a climactic confrontation between Heflin and Stanwyck that she discovers he never knew she killed her aunt until *that* moment!)

Most of the story covers the events of a few days following the adult Heflin's return to Iverstown, where he again becomes involved in the lives of Stanwyck, now the wealthy owner of the town's chief industry, and Douglas, whom she married only to insure his silence about her crime, and is now backing for mayor. Before the film's close, Heflin is caught up in their miserable lives, is nearly killed by hoodlums hired by Douglas to intimidate him, and is sexually toyed with by a coolly seductive Stanwyck, who would as soon kill him as kiss him. It's a taut game of wits between these two well-matched people.

Later, on a hilltop where they've parked, Stanwyck spills out her cold heart to him: "If only you hadn't left town. I had no one to turn to. It would have been so different if you hadn't run away." When she learns he has just discovered the truth about her aunt's death, she savagely attacks him with a burning stick, but

CALIFORNIA (1947). With Ray Milland

he pins her arms back and they kiss. Nowhere in the film is Martha Ivers's deadly ambivalent personality better exemplified. Finally, obsessed with disposing of the useless Douglas to make room for a future with Heflin, whom she sexually desires, she urges the latter to kill her husband before he can recover from a drunken fall down their sweeping staircase. He turns on her with bitter revulsion ("You're so sick you don't even know the difference between right and wrong anymore"), and ignoring her threat to shoot him, he walks out of their lives, saying, "I feel sorry for you—both of you."

Faced with the discovery of a murder to which they were party eighteen years earlier, Stanwyck and Douglas solve their problems with a double suicide, as Heflin goes off with Lizabeth Scott, the attractive parolee who has hovered at the edges of this sordid tale.

Thanks to a cunning collaboration between screenwriter and director, this improbable melodrama proves quite gripping right through to its double-barreled finale. One critic called Stanwyck's Martha "twice the hard-boiled, lustful vixen that she played in *Double Indemnity*," and also praised Heflin for his performance, his first following war service.

Having perhaps topped herself with this portrayal of ruthless villainy, Stanwyck now turned to the

Western with *California* (1947). The actress' first Technicolor movie, *California* presents her as a cynical, saloon-singing, poker-playing adventuress of the Old West, who meets her match in frontiersman Ray Milland in the gold-rush days of the Forty-Niners. John Farrow directed this expensive, brawling movie, emphasizing the rough-and-tumble aspects of the Frank Butler-Theodore Strauss screenplay.

Stanwyck sets the picture's tone with her diverting "entrance," when she's tossed out of her hotel, bag and baggage, into a mud puddle by the town's more "respectable" ladies. "Thank you," she responds quietly through her teeth, not giving anyone the satisfaction of seeing her defeated. Amid her subsequent love-hate relationship with the ungentlemanly Milland, she threatens to rub his face in the mud, and is rewarded with a hard slap across the face—an offbeat reversal of the *usual* man-woman scene.

Stanwyck looks great in her Edith Head period costumes, but she's understandably ill-at-ease delivering (in a dubbed voice) a pair of mediocre E.Y. Harburg-Earl Robinson song numbers, *Lily-Ay-O* and *Goodbye, Said My Heart*.

Back at Warners, she played an overage Nancy Drew in *Cry Wolf* (1947), director Peter Godfrey's minor but effective melodrama involving a frightened heroine with a strange family on a mysterious, rambling estate that obviously contains some dread secret. Errol Flynn seemed oddly cast as the enigmatic head of this household, with Geraldine Brooks as an intrigu-

CRY WOLF (1947). With Errol Flynn and John Ridgely

THE OTHER LOVE (1947). With David Niven

ing neurotic whose untimely death prevents the revelation of what she might know.

Catherine Turney's adaptation of Marjorie Carleton's novel does little to make the unlikely events convincing, though Peter Godfrey, composer Franz Waxman and cinematographer Carl Guthrie make a valiant attempt to create the proper atmosphere of mystery and suspense. For Stanwyck there's quite an athletic workout, requiring her to climb fences, travel up and down in dumbwaiters, navigate along high rooftops and climb through skylights to drop into the rooms below. In a plot that would do credit to Carolyn Keene, there is little time for thoughts of romance and, despite Flynn's presence, it is perhaps just as well. The melodrama proceeds to its illogical conclusion, unhampered by the convention of more romantic movie thrillers.

With this melodrama, Stanwyck ended her association with Warner Bros. Although she had succeeded in getting Jack Warner to obtain the rights to Ayn Rand's novel, *The Fountainhead*, especially for her, the coveted role of tempestuous Dominique Francon was taken away at the eleventh hour when that film's director, King Vidor, decided that Stanwyck lacked the requisite sex appeal—a quality that Patricia

Neal (who got the role) had in spades. This was a bitter blow to Stanwyck, and it is interesting to note that this harsh and abrupt cast change took place shortly before the career reversal of Warners' former top dramatic star, Bette Davis, given impetus by *Beyond the Forest*, Vidor's subsequent Warners film.

In *The Other Love* (1947), an Enterprise Studios production released by United Artists, Stanwyck is back among the familiar trappings of soap opera. Harry Brown and Ladislas Fodor collaborated to turn Erich Maria Remarque's short story "Beyond" into a dark romance about a tubercular concert pianist (Stanwyck) who rejects the love of her doctor (David Niven), at a fancy Swiss mountain sanitarium, when she discovers the gravity of her illness. Convinced that he merely pities her, she runs away to Monte Carlo for a last fling with a playboy (Richard Conte), though she eventually returns to marry her doctor and await her inevitable demise with serenity.

David Lewis' production surrounds his stars with lavish settings, and Miklos Rozsa's music (laced with selections from the Great Masters) underlines the romantic atmosphere. Under Andre de Toth's direction, it's all very lush and hollow, and Stanwyck somehow never quite convinces that she is dying of a dread disease. This modern Camille appears just a bit too healthy and energetic to succumb to that cough. The cast gives it a good try, but *The Other Love* doesn't ring true.

Back at Paramount, Barbara Stanwyck appeared briefly, as herself, along with almost all of that studio's stars and other contract players, in *Variety Girl* (1947), a slimly plotted tribute to the philanthropic work of the nation's Variety Clubs on behalf of underprivileged youngsters. Stanwyck's scene, com-

VARIETY GIRL (1947). With Joan Caulfield

B.F.'S DAUGHTER (1948). With Van Heflin

ing near the start of the film, consists of explaining to Joan Caulfield how Variety Clubs first started.

During 1947 she and Taylor took a much-needed European vacation (some said it was an attempt to solve marital problems), and when they returned, Stanwyck reported to work at MGM for *B.F.'s Daughter*, a Luther Davis adaptation of the J.P. Marquand novel. In this drama about a tycoon's offspring whose wealth and headstrong nature interfere with her romantic life, Stanwyck was guided by Robert Z. Leonard, long one of Norma Shearer's favorite directors. For this film, and to keep up with the changing times, Stanwyck cut her shoulder-length hair to a well-sculptured bob of the type Shearer herself had maintained during the final years of her career. One thing she refused to alter, however, was the color of her hair, which, at forty, was showing increasing wisps of gray.

In *B.F.'s Daughter*, Stanwyck played a doer married to a thinker (Van Heflin), who finds his wife attempting to recast him in the mold of herself and her strong-willed father (Charles Coburn). Though set in the Depression years, there was little evidence of this in the star's New Look wardrobe by Irene. The film was glossy, chic and rather hollow, though an excellent cast

SORRY, WRONG NUMBER (1948). With Burt Lancaster

SORRY, WRONG NUMBER (1948). As Leona Stevenson

made results look better than they were. But the critical fraternity was unimpressed.

Back at Paramount, Stanwyck was far better served by *Sorry, Wrong Number*, which Lucille Fletcher had revised and expanded from her famed radio suspense play that had provided Agnes Moorehead with one of her finest half hours in 1943. On the air, it had been a tour de force for its leading lady, centering on a wealthy, bedridden hypochondriac who overhears, on crossed telephone wires, two men plotting the contract murder of a woman later that night. Alone in her Manhattan townhouse, she is merely shocked, then irritated, as she tries to tell the phone company, then the police, all without success. Her annoyance turns to terror when she realizes that the facts of the murder plot point to the identity of the victim— *herself!* As her desperation increases, the murderer closes in and carries out his deadly assignment. When the victim's phone rings, the killer lifts the receiver, says "Sorry, wrong number," and hangs up.

Developing this 22-minute tale of mounting terror into an 89-minute motion picture required extensive work, and Miss Fletcher's screenplay, while failing to please some critics, intrigued others with the complex web of story and character entanglements she wove to draw a logical background for the murder plot. Indeed, the film's very structure is extremely intricate itself, as a current event leads to a flashback—within a flashback. All of this rather cumbersome exposition is rendered interesting by director Anatole Litvak, who never loses control of his sprawling plot details, while always continuing to build the requisite suspense.

Although Stanwyck spends much of her footage in bed with the phone, many scenes from the character's past tell us about the woman's selfish and neurotic dominance of her rough-diamond husband (Burt Lancaster), for whom she had secured employment in her father's vast drug empire. Unlike the radio play, this woman is hardly sympathetic, so there is little that Stanwyck can do to make one care for her fate. Instead, she must work on the woman's gradual change from initial shock at hearing a murder plot to outraged frustration and mounting fear as she learns that her desperate husband has hired men to murder her for the insurance money he needs to pay a debt to the mob. In the ironic ending Miss Fletcher devised for the movie, we learn that circumstances no longer make it necessary for the woman to be murdered. But by the time the husband gets to her on the phone and she informs him of this, it is too late to

THE LADY GAMBLES (1949). With Stephen McNally

prevent the murder. And the film ends as did the radio script.

Sorry, Wrong Number is not an easy film to carry off with success, but Litvak manages it well, with the aid of atmospheric settings, Sol Polito's moody photography, George White's sharp editing and the Franz Waxman background score. Unlike Moorehead's performance, Stanwyck is often off-screen while the camera explores other aspects of the tangled plot. But when she is on-camera, Stanwyck is flawless. Her best scenes are those closest to the radio play, in which she eloquently conveys the growing horror of an irritable neurotic whose annoyance turns to well-justified fear—then desperation. For these scenes, Litvak very considerately gave Stanwyck the choice of shooting the necessary twelve days in the bedroom set all at once—in sequence—or, to make it easier on her, alternate them with her other scenes. She chose the former approach, which accounts for the conviction with which we watch her gradual progress from bored, well-groomed irritation, coping with a rare night alone in the summer heat, to disheveled terror as fear activates her adrenalin and replaces her concern for the pills and medicines she swallows for her self-induced "heart condition."

The critics had high praise for her performance, with a particular nod to her harrowing battle with that telephone, and she was awarded her fourth (and last, to date) Academy Award nomination. But again the award went to someone else—Jane Wyman for her affecting portrayal of the deaf-mute in *Johnny Belinda*. Two years later, Stanwyck repeated *Sorry, Wrong Number* herself for an hour-long live performance on *Lux Radio Theatre*. A 1954 television adaptation was considerably less successful, featuring Shelley Winters as a hypochondriac so obnoxious that her imminent demise came not a moment too soon.

A different sort of emotional workout was required of Barbara Stanwyck in her next film, originally called *Gambling Lady*, although it bore no other relationship to her 1934 Warners film of that name. Finally retitled *The Lady Gambles*, this Universal-International melodrama presented her as a happily married newspaperman's wife, whose addiction to gambling destroys her marriage to Robert Preston, reduces her to a B-girl in sleazy casinos and, finally, to an ambulance case in an emergency hospital, after she's beaten up during a back-alley crap game. Her husband is sent for and, after an unsuccessful suicide attempt, the ex-gambling lady appears set for a brighter future.

Stanwyck plays this demanding role to the hilt and, unlike her menaced invalid in *Sorry, Wrong Number*, in *The Lady Gambles* she's never far from view. Forced to cope with a Roy Huggins script that mixed in some sketchy Freudian explanations for her addiction, Stanwyck nevertheless tore into the part with a conviction that virtually *compelled* viewers to believe, unless they chose to analyze the plot afterwards. Aided by some authentic Las Vegas locations, director Michael Gordon contrives to keep *The Lady Gambles* a notch or two above the average psychological soap opera, and he's greatly assisted by the smooth supporting performances of Stephen McNally as the slick pro gambler who encourages Stanwyck's initial fling at roulette, Edith Barrett, as her clinging-vine spinster sister, and John Hoyt, as the cynical doctor who helps give her the will to live. Stanwyck's work garnered excellent notices, and one critic even likened her display of gambling fever to Ray Milland's battle with the bottle in *The Lost Weekend*.

THE MIDDLE YEARS: SUDS AND PROGRAMMERS

Barbara Stanwyck spent most of 1949 before the MGM and Paramount cameras in a steady succession of dramas and melodramas.

In *Thelma Jordan* (also known as *The File on Thelma Jordan*), Stanwyck is again involved with crime, as a predatory female who lures a naïve, married assistant DA (Wendell Corey) into an intricate plot of murder and deceit (she's killed her wealthy aunt). The turgid Ketti Frings script challenged Stanwyck to convince an audience that she could be both a gangster's trollop and a rich spinster's companion, and then had her make a climactic revelation that she was, in fact, a schizoid murderess. And although she gave it the wholehearted effort of a real pro, the task was as impossible for her as it was for director Robert Siodmak to build action and suspense out of a dull and unlikely plot. Paramount kept *Thelma Jordan* on the shelf for some time, and when it finally surfaced in early 1950, it disappeared rather quickly.

For Paramount's *No Man of Her Own* (no relation to that studio's 1932 Clark Gable-Carole Lombard film of the same name), Stanwyck again teamed with director Mitchell Leisen, this time in a drama that was a far cry from their *Remember the Night*. If its title smacks of soap opera, *No Man of Her Own* at least affords Stanwyck plenty of opportunity to suffer in the Joan Crawford-Bette Davis vein. She plays Helen Ferguson, the pregnant but unmarried girlfriend of villainous Lyle Bettger (in his movie debut), who rejects her. Involved in a train wreck, she assumes the identity of Patrice Harkness, the widow of a dead war hero, who is killed in the accident. Stanwyck seizes this opportunity to impersonate the dead woman, and because the husband's parents had never met their daughter-in-law, she is successful at building a new life. Eventually she falls in love with the dead girl's brother-in-law (John Lund). Her happiness ends, however, when Bettger turns up, aware of her deception and intent on blackmail. After much trouble for the principals, this blackguard is killed off (by another woman altogether), paving the way for a happy ending.

The basis for this display of lurid melodrama (known during production as *The Lie*) is a William Irish novel called *I Married a Dead Man*. Although Sally Benson and Catherine Turney share screen credit —and bear the brunt of the blame for the movie's plethora of coincidences and clichés—director Leisen later disclosed that most of

THELMA JORDAN (1950). With Wendell Corey

the work was his, with Turney's work present only in the opening scenes. ("We threw Sally Benson's version out entirely.")

East Side, West Side returned her to the handsome production trappings of MGM and a starring role in Isobel Lennart's adaptation of Marcia Davenport's popular novel of romance and marital infidelity in New York society. Stanwyck plays the cool, beautiful and well-born wife of philandering James Mason, whose flagrant affair with model Ava Gardner causes Stanwyck much anguish and draws her close to sympathetic Van Heflin. Mervyn LeRoy directed this slick "woman's picture" for all it was worth, and makes it appear much better than it actually is. A very subdued, well-mannered Stanwyck's best moments occur in scenes with Van Heflin (their acting styles blend well), and with other actresses—one in which she confronts Gardner (who, unexpectedly, holds her own with Stanwyck in an exciting exchange of barely controlled animosity), and another in which she attempts, against her better judgment, to assure her friend, Nancy Davis, that her marriage to Mason is not in trouble.

Back at Paramount for *The Furies*, in the blonde wig which was becoming something of a trademark for Stanwyck in a "stop-at-nothing" character, she joined an expert cast, topped by Walter Huston (in his last role), Wendell Corey and Judith Anderson. It was a sprawling outdoor saga with Freudian overtones in which a willful, ruthless Stanwyck (aggressively named Vance Jeffords) guides a cattle empire for her widower-father (Huston)—until jealousy and revenge (she loathes Judith Anderson, the intended new bride he brings home) split them apart.

Directed by Anthony Mann, this Hal Wallis production was big in every way but one—it was filmed in old-fashioned black-and-white which, considering the colorful characters and locations (near Tucson, Arizona), makes it hard to understand why Wallis vetoed Technicolor on a major production in 1950. For its day, the Charles Schnee script (from a Niven Busch novel) was quite adult, exploring the almost sexual ties between father and daughter, whose combined strengths are formidable, particularly as portrayed by Huston and Stanwyck. (Their mutual off-screen respect and rapport is reflected in their scenes together.) Judith Anderson, always a forceful and vital actress, is a strong opponent to Stanwyck for Huston's affections, and one of *The Furies*' most emotion-charged scenes is the one in which an enraged Vance alienates her adored father by disfiguring the scheming widow with a well-aimed

NO MAN OF HER OWN (1950). With John Lund

EAST SIDE, WEST SIDE (1949). With Ava Gardner

pair of scissors.

But the film also has its romantic moments, involving our iron-willed heroine with two men, a dashing Mexican squatter (Gilbert Roland), who claims rights to her land (and whom her father hangs), and a gambler (Wendell Corey), who teams up with her to wrest the ranch away from her father—a revenge plan halted by the old man's untimely death at the hands of the squatter's mother (Blanche Yurka).

Interesting in prospect, but dismally disappointing in result was the idea of teaming Barbara Stanwyck with Clark Gable—the first time since 1931's *Night Nurse*—for MGM's *To Please a Lady* (1950). Produced and directed by the veteran Clarence Brown, it was a romantic drama whose battling protagonists are a tough, uncompromising columnist and an equally ruthless racing driver. Their off-again, on-again romance is punctuated with return visits to the race track, where the movie often turns dull from a plethora of routine action footage. By the same token, more red-blooded audiences could only become restless and impatient with the script's silly romantic nip-ups, although, to their credit, writers Barré Lyndon and Marge Decker turned out some admirably fast and flip dialogue.

After this film, Stanwyck flew to Rome to join Robert Taylor on the set of the spectacular *Quo Vadis*,

THE FURIES (1950). With Walter Huston and Judith Anderson

whose lengthy production schedule had provided their longest—and most telling—separation since World War II. She was with him six weeks, and it was presumed that they had patched up any problems. But in December, after Taylor's return, they issued the following joint statement: "In the past few years, because of professional requirements, we have been separated just too often and too long. Our sincere and continued efforts to maintain our marriage have failed. We are deeply disappointed that we could not solve our problems. We really tried. There will be a California divorce. Neither of us has any other romantic interest whatsoever."

At this unhappy juncture of her life, Stanwyck's career slowed considerably and, during 1951 and 1952, she only had one film released each year. *The Man With a Cloak* (1951) is a good little turn-of-the-century thriller about a plot to murder an aged millionaire (Louis Calhern) by his housekeeper (Stanwyck) and butler (Joe De Santis). The deliberately paced plot also features the old man's French granddaughter (Leslie Caron) and a mysterious stranger (Joseph Cotten) who might be Edgar Allan Poe. In handsome period costumes by Walter Plunkett and a dark wig, Stanwyck had little to do but be attractively sinister and regal.

TO PLEASE A LADY (1950). With Clark Gable

THE MAN WITH A CLOAK (1951). With Margaret Wycherly and Joe De Santis

Her return to RKO for Fritz Lang's emotion-charged *Clash by Night* (1952) was more fortuitous. In this Alfred Hayes reworking of Clifford Odets' 1941 stage flop, Stanwyck took on a role originated by Tallulah Bankhead, with Paul Douglas and Robert Ryan as her leading men—and an up-and-coming blonde actress named Marilyn Monroe in a subsidiary role.

Stanwyck's role in this film is one of her best. She plays Mae Doyle, a cynical but frustrated woman who returns to the California fishing community of her youth to share a house with her brother Joe (Keith Andes). "Home," she tells Joe's girlfriend Peggy (Marilyn Monroe), "is where ya come when ya run outa places." Mae is courted by, and marries, down-to-earth fisherman Jerry D'Amato (Paul Douglas), but she finds herself attracted to Earl Pfeiffer (Robert Ryan), a complex, intimidating misogynist. Restless with Jerry, she has an affair with Earl which ends in a violent confrontation between the two men. Finally Mae and Jerry are reconciled after Mae has learned to be content with her lot.

CLASH BY NIGHT (1952). With Robert Ryan

JEOPARDY (1953). With Barry Sullivan

Stanwyck's Mae is as complex as Robert Ryan's cunningly charming Earl, allowing her past battles with life and love to surface from time to time in cathartic bits and pieces. For a 1952 film, *Clash by Night* sometimes waxes rather steamy, particularly in the morning-after scene between Stanwyck and Ryan. About to leave Stanwyck's house after passing out drunkenly on her sofa, he approaches her, pulls her into his arms and kisses her hard. She immediately resists (she's a married woman now), but then begins to respond, finally abandoning any concern of discovery as she impulsively runs her hands beneath his undershirt.

Recalling *Clash by Night*, director Fritz Lang reports, "Working with Barbara Stanwyck was one of the greatest pleasures of my career. She's fantastic, unbelievable, and I liked her tremendously. When Marilyn missed her lines —which she did constantly— Barbara never said a word." *Clash by Night* is a powerful downbeat drama. Critical reaction was mixed, and the film's box-office success is probably due more to the presence of Marilyn Monroe (who, despite her rather small role, got very big billing) than to any other factor.

On February 26, 1952, some months before the release of *Clash by Night*, Stanwyck's divorce from

ALL I DESIRE (1953).
As Naomi Murdoch

Taylor became final. Two years later, he married the German actress Ursula Thiess, a union that endured until his death in 1969. To date Barbara Stanwyck has never remarried. In a 1958 interview in the *Los Angeles Times*, she said, "I didn't get married to get divorced. It took me a long time to get over it. Unlike my divorce from Fay. I wasn't the least upset by that one. I had stood his colossal ego and everything else as long as I could."

After the divorce, Stanwyck moved out of the home she shared with Taylor, and Buck Mack went with her. Her adopted son Dion served in the Army, stationed in Germany, and in 1957 he married a Las Vegas showgirl. Over the years, he and Stanwyck became estranged, and their relationship is a subject about which she now chooses to remain silent.

In 1953 Stanwyck compensated for her recent dearth of movies by appearing in no less than five films. Returning to MGM, she enjoyed a strenuous emotional workout in *Jeopardy*, an unusual little program suspense yarn directed by John Sturges, who had already scored at that studio with *Mystery Street* and *Kind Lady*. Mel Dinelli's taut script derives its excitement from the plight of Helen Stilwin (Stanwyck), on a Mexican camping holiday with husband Doug (Barry Sullivan) and son Bobby (Lee Aaker). Freeing his son from the rotting timbers of an abandoned jetty, Doug himself becomes trapped, as the tide moves in. Driving for help, Helen encounters Lawson (Ralph Meeker), an escaped convict, who forces her to drive him away from pursuing police. In a desperate effort to get help to her husband, Helen agrees to give her husband's clothing and identification to him—and even herself—if he will help her free Doug from the prospect of imminent drowning. Lawson agrees and they return to the beach, where Doug's head is just above the water.

Doug is freed, but only after Helen fights Lawson desperately to keep him from leaving with her husband's identification. Lawson, lost in admiration of Helen's courage, goes off alone.

The story's melodrama is so well handled by Sturges' fast-paced direction that he holds the film to a mere 69 minutes, with no time left for audience boredom. Of Stanwyck, Sturges says, "Making a pic-

TITANIC (1953). With Robert Wagner, Audrey Dalton, Allyn Joslyn, Harper Carter, Clifton Webb, and Charles Fitzsimmons

BLOWING WILD (1953). With Gary Cooper

ture with Missy is such a stimulating and productive experience, it's hard to think how it could be better." *Jeopardy*, a film for which MGM had little hope, gathered some very complimentary reviews and turned into a box-office "sleeper."

Back at Universal, Stanwyck returned to period clothing to play Naomi Murdoch, a fallen woman with a good heart in *All I Desire*, a James Gunn-Robert Blees adaptation of Carol Ryrie Brink's short novel, *Stopover*. In this costume tear-jerker, directed by Douglas Sirk, she played a mother who, following a small-town indiscretion with another man (Lyle Bettger) ten years earlier, had left her schoolteacher husband (Richard Carlson) and three young children to seek a career on the wicked stage. Now, she's back for a brief visit to see her younger daughter (Lori Nelson) perform in the school graduation play. Since Naomi's return stirs up unexpected feelings for her estranged husband, as well as unwanted attentions from her ex-lover, there's a lot of tears and soul-searching before an ending in which it looks as though Naomi will

THE MOONLIGHTER (1953). With Fred MacMurray

leave her dubious show-business pursuits to resume her former life as wife and mother. (In the book, Naomi goes back to her chosen profession.)

All I Desire is a modest programmer, designed for the distaff audiences which producers now realized were the larger portion of Stanwyck's fans. Ross Hunter's production values were very respectable (and this was before his glossy Technicolored remakes of past hits), and so was his cast. But, faced with the clichés of this adaptation and its altered conclusion, it remains for Barbara Stanwyck's down-to-earth delineation of a "bad" woman turning "good" to carry the film off.

20th Century-Fox's *Titanic* (1953) is far more successful as a re-creation of an historic event than as personal drama, although there are a number of excellent performances from a cast headed by Stanwyck and Clifton Webb (as a socially prominent couple on the brink of divorce) and featuring Thelma Ritter (unexpectedly dolled up in the height of 1912 fashions), Richard Basehart, Brian Aherne and Robert Wagner. Made of many intermingled minor dramas, this spectacular Charles Brackett production is very well handled by director Jean Negulesco, who manages to create and maintain suspense, despite the fact that nearly all audiences already knew the tragic fate of the ship and her passengers. Consequently, *Titanic* is in no small way indebted to its Charles Brackett-Walter Reisch-Richard Breen screenplay, for which Oscars were awarded. But the film's almost frightening realism is also a tribute to art directors Lyle Wheeler and Maurice Ransford, who created the ship and its enemy icebergs in the studio's outdoor tank. Filming the final scenes of escape from the tilted, sinking ship was not easy, and Stanwyck recalls swinging some 47 feet up in the air in a dangling lifeboat on a bitter cold night with masses of humanity below in the agitated water: "I thought of the men and women who had been through this thing in our time. We were re-creating an actual tragedy and I burst into tears. I shook with great racking sobs and couldn't stop."

For *Blowing Wild* (1953), Stanwyck returned to Warners—and a reunion with her old co-star Gary Cooper, though in a vehicle far below the class of their previous films together. Accepting a role that Lauren Bacall had rejected, Stanwyck was once more a "bad" woman, playing Marina Conway, the scheming, faithless wife of an oil driller (Anthony Quinn), who is anxious to resume an old affair with her husband's partner (Gary Cooper). Stanwyck spends most of the film making a play for Cooper, and when he appears to be more interested in a stranded showgirl (Ruth Roman), she disposes of hubby by shoving him into some pounding oil-well machinery. Eventually, she gets blown to bits herself by dynamite, after screaming at Cooper, "I committed murder to get you! Murder!"

This highly charged and utterly incredible romantic melodrama was hardly the right material for stars of the collective maturity of Cooper, Quinn and Stanwyck, and Hugo Fregonese's direction of a dreadful Philip Yordan script couldn't help. Capping the whole filmed-in-Mexico fiasco was Frankie Laine's bellowing voice on the soundtrack, rendering lyrics like "Marina mine, set me free," backed by a chanting female chorus.

Warners' Natural Vision 3-D Western, *The Moonlighter* (1953), was certainly no better. Again Stanwyck was matched with a co-star (Fred MacMurray) with whom she had shared some excellent scripts, and it was beginning to look as if several great careers were petering out that year in shameful disasters. The studio didn't even think enough of this gimmicky oater to film it in Warnercolor, and Niven Busch's sluggish, downbeat script, about cattle rustlers and bank robbers, offered scant opportunities for director Roy Rowland and his cast, although Stanwyck seemed to enjoy riding horses, handling guns, and performing as many of her own stunts as Warners would allow her.

THE QUEEN: DRAWING ROOM TO SAGEBRUSH

Of Barbara Stanwyck's three 1954 movies, one—MGM's *Executive Suite*—was a superior drama, worthy of its high-powered cast (William Holden, Fredric March, June Allyson, Walter Pidgeon, Shelley Winters, Paul Douglas and Nina Foch). Based on Cameron Hawley's popular novel about a corporate power struggle following the sudden death of a business executive, this expert Ernest Lehman screenplay gave director Robert Wise a splendid opportunity to show the skill with which he could fuse a top-drawer movie when the elements were as positive as they were here.

An ensemble film, *Executive Suite* affords each of its stars a chance to shine in his/her separate segments, and Stanwyck is impressive as neurotic Julia Tredway, daughter of the corporation's founder and embittered mistress of the just-deceased tycoon, whose death has robbed her of her every reason for living. But she's a major stockholder in the company, and her presence is not only required at the obligatory board meeting, but she must be handled with kid gloves. Stanwyck's most explosive scenes are with Holden, who deliberately forces her to unleash her pent-up emotions on him. In their only joint effort since *Golden Boy*, these two pros respond so well to each other's acting skills that one could wish they had found further opportunities to co-star. For Stanwyck, this was her best MGM picture, and her last (to date) unqualified first-class motion picture. From here on, reflecting the changing tastes of filmgoers, and the sharply narrowing film opportunities for aging actresses, her roles would have to be chiefly in Westerns, thrillers and grade-B soap operas.

Witness to Murder (1954) was an independent Chester Erskine production, directed by Roy Rowland and released through United Artists. In this low-budget, implausible melodrama, Stanwyck plays a career woman who sees a neighbor (George Sanders) commit murder across the intervening courtyard one night, but can't get anyone to believe her, including an otherwise sympathetic police detective (Gary Merrill). Before the harrowing cliff-hanging finale, Stanwyck turns detective, narrowly escapes being murdered herself, and is committed to an institution for a time, convinced she is losing her mind. All the while, she continues to fear Sanders—with good reason, as it turns out. Because of the professional competence of its stars,

EXECUTIVE SUITE (1954). With William Holden

Witness to Murder holds some interest, though it's little more than a cheap programmer.

During a 1965 interview for the *Toronto Telegram*, Stanwyck spoke candidly to interviewer Clyde Gilmour about making this class of film, in which she now seemed to specialize during the 1950s: "The answer is simply that you make a horrible mistake. You get taken in by what seems like a basically good idea and a sort of rough, temporary screenplay and you sign on to do the picture without ever having seen a completed script. Within one week after the start of shooting, everybody on the set knows that the thing is just not jelling. But by that time, you're hooked. So you do the best you can—and you privately hope that nobody goes to see it."

At RKO, continuing in this unfortunate vein, Stanwyck, agreeing to cover her gray hair with a wig, now paired with Ronald Reagan, whose career had also seen better days, in a Western entitled *Cattle Queen of Montana* (1955), her first Technicolor film since *California*, eight years earlier. There was nothing new to this outdoor tale of Indians battling the encroachment of white settlers, but Stanwyck, as Sierra Nevada Jones, played vigorously and endured numerous physical discomforts (including bathing in a frigid mountain lake) in the interests of authenticity. Allan Dwan's slack direction was of little help to a negligible script, but John Alton's photography showed Stanwyck to good advantage.

In Columbia's *The Violent Men* (1954), filmed under the title *Rough Company*, Stanwyck was once more back in a major production with important co-stars (Glenn Ford, Edward G. Robinson) and top production values (Technicolor, Cinema-Scope). It's an intermittently interesting Western, unevenly directed by Rudolph Maté, but enhanced by colorful location photography (Burnett Guffey and W. Howard Greene). In a blonde wig (cueing the audience that she's not to be trusted), Stanwyck plays a scheming woman married to crippled rancher Edward G. Robinson, while cheating on the side with virile Brian Keith who, in turn, disturbs her by dallying with Lita Milan ("Oh, Cole, don't cheapen yourself! Send that Mexican girl away!").

The Violent Men has its share of action scenes, as relief from the family backbiting, and in a rousing climax, Stanwyck attempts to kill Robinson as their ranch burns. However, she and Keith meet vio-

WITNESS TO MURDER (1954). With Gary Merrill and George Sanders

CATTLE QUEEN OF MONTANA (1955). With Ronald Reagan

lent ends soon thereafter, while Robinson and the film's romantic pair (Glenn Ford and Dianne Foster) are among the few survivors. Next to Stanwyck's other films of this period, *The Violent Men* really looks like a super-Western.

Another collaboration of producer Benedict Bogeaus and director Allan Dwan, *Escape to Burma* (1955), now reunited Stanwyck with her *Clash by Night* co-star, Robert Ryan. They would have been well advised to forget the whole project before it went into production, for this musty romantic jungle melodrama, set in Burma, mixes its stars with elephants, tigers and jungle bandits in and around the teak plantation owned by Stanwyck, and the results are very embarrassing for all concerned. The cliché-ridden script by Talbot Jennings and Hobart Donavan had little to offer a mid-1950s audience, and Dwan's efforts to give his film pace were futile. As Stanwyck later remarked, "The animals were better than the picture!"

Back at Universal, she again participated in a Douglas Sirk film for producer Ross Hunter, *There's Always Tomorrow* (1956). This was an old Ursula Parrott story about an unappreciated husband (Fred MacMurray), whose wife (Joan Bennett) neglects him for their children (William Reynolds, Gigi Perreau and Judy Nugent) and paves the way to his rekindling an

THE VIOLENT MEN (1955). With Lita Milan

old romance (Stanwyck). In 1934 it had provided a vehicle for Frank Morgan, with Lois Wilson as his wife and British Binnie Barnes, in her American film debut, as the other woman.

The remake, well acted by a highly competent cast, was a conventional triangle drama about a marriage strengthened by crisis. But Bernard C. Schoenfeld's screenplay couldn't resist such hoary dialogue as Stanwyck's telling MacMurray, as they become very close again after twenty years apart, "I didn't mean for this to happen." To which he replies, inevitably, "But it *did* happen." Then, after a confrontation between children and mistress, in which she lectures them about their duties to their father, she advises his wife, "Treat your man better, or next time you may lose him for good." And off she goes, back to her lonely but glamorous life as a New York fashion designer. *There's Always Tomorrow* is a respectable little soap opera with few pretensions.

But Republic's 1956 Western, *The Maverick Queen*, produced in Trucolor and a short-lived widescreen process called Naturama, is something else. If not quite as "super" as that studio's 1954 *Johnny Guitar*, this hokey take of the Wyoming Territory when it was rough and dangerous is at least entertaining. In a stylish dark wig and a wardrobe mixing outdoor riding togs with fancy period gowns, Stanwyck is at her toughest as Kit Banion, a woman who "did what I had to do to get where I am." Since she is owner and proprietor of the Maverick Queen Saloon in a county lively with the activities of such legendary outlaws as Butch Cassidy (Howard Petrie) and the Sundance Kid (Scott Brady), the movie doesn't have much chance to bore its audience.

Early on, plainclothes Pinkerton agent Barry Sullivan shows up at Stanwyck's place, and the plot immediately makes it easy for him as the lady conveniently offers, "How about a job dealing faro? One of my boys left last week." Despite a growing affection for Sullivan, Stanwyck is hard and uncompromising with everyone else, though she reveals she's "part of a gang run by Butch Cassidy."

Before the film's slam-bang climax, she softens and falls hard for Sullivan, but justice will out and in a shoot-out, she dies in his arms.

Whenever *The Maverick Queen* comes close to being taken seriously, the voice of Joni James jolts one back to bemused reality with a recurring sound-track ballad that fondles such deathless lyrics as: "Oh, the Maverick Queen, the Maverick Queen . . . She could steal your heart away." And then helpfully warns us: "There was trouble ahead for the Maverick Queen."

Filmed around Silverton, Col-

ESCAPE TO BURMA (1955). With Peter Coe, Robert Ryan, and David Farrar

THERE'S ALWAYS TOMORROW (1956). With William Reynolds and Gigi Perreau

THE MAVERICK QUEEN (1956). With Scott Brady and Barry Sullivan

orado, *The Maverick Queen* boasts fine outdoor footage and, under Joseph Kane's direction, some lively action scenes, with a properly hardened Stanwyck playing for all she's worth. But this alleged Zane Grey story (in reality, merely Republic's flacks hoodwinking the public) wasn't worthy of her, and only the energy and enthusiasm of her performance make one, momentarily, *think* that it is.

In prospect, MGM's *Somewhere I'll Find Him*, casting Stanwyck opposite James Cagney, sounds far more prestigious, but this was not the case. Just before its release, this slow, sudsy drama's title was altered to *These Wilder Years*, in a vain attempt to increase its selling power. Stanwyck's role was secondary to Cagney's in this Frank Fenton script about an aging millionaire tycoon who takes time off from his busy life to trace the present whereabouts of an illegitimate son he fathered and repudiated twenty years earlier. Stanwyck is the kindly but high-principled head of an adoption agency whose opposition

THESE WILDER YEARS (1956). With James Cagney and Lewis Martin

precipitates a legal battle. Eventually, Cagney is reunited with his son, but realizes that the boy is better off with his adopted parents, and he compensates his guilt feelings by adopting an unwed teen-age mother (Betty Lou Keim) whom he had met earlier at the agency.

Neither the script nor Roy Rowland's direction do anything to raise *These Wilder Years* above the level of sentimental daytime TV drama, and the best Stanwyck and Cagney can do is carry off their roles with professional ease.

The actress had far more to do in her next film, *Crime of Passion* (1957). Here, she is once again a strong-willed career woman—a newspaper reporter—who gives up her own career to marry policeman Sterling Hayden, whose bland personality and dull friends soon drive her to frenzy with impatience for his career. The film is not very far along before Stanwyck enjoys her first tirade, screaming at him, "Don't you have any *ambition?!*"

She is so consumed with the need for an outlet for her energy and redirected career ambitions that she connives to get her husband promoted, and ends up destroying not only his career, but her marriage and her future—when, following an abortive extramarital affair with his boss (Raymond Burr), she shoots and kills him. She is a veritable modern Lady Macbeth, though the sleazy quality of the enterprise is not helped by Jo Eisinger's contrived and unbelievable screenplay or Gerd Oswald's pedestrian direction. Nor could a noisy Miklos Rozsa score give it any class.

In *Trooper Hook* (1957), she teamed for the sixth and last time with Joel McCrea in a Charles Marquis Warren Western with an offbeat theme. In a Cavalry attack on an Apache village, the sergeant-leader (McCrea) finds a white woman (Stanwyck) living among the squaws. It develops that she's been there for years, ever since she was abducted from her home and husband, and has a five-year-old half-breed son by the cruel Apache chief (Rodolfo Acosta). They take her back to civilization and her husband (John Dehner), who refuses to accept the child. But then the Apache chief sets out to retrieve his boy, and after a lot of contrived action, husband and Indian chief are killed off, leaving Stanwyck and her child to find solace with the more tolerant McCrea. The black-and-white film's budget was low, but writer-

CRIME OF PASSION (1957). With Sterling Hayden

TROOPER HOOK (1957). With Terry Lawrence and Joel McCrea

director Warren had some original ideas, and backed by a good cast, McCrea and Stanwyck deliver nicely understated performances.

Stanwyck was back in the saddle again for Samuel Fuller's *Forty Guns* (1957), a complex outdoor action drama filmed in black-and-white CinemaScope, which made her gray hair look blonde. Fuller wrote, produced and directed this rugged tale of Old Tombstone, with Stanwyck as the ruthless boss of Cochise County who made her own laws with the backing of forty armed horsemen. The film's main romantic thread involves a strange attraction between her and federal peace officer Barry Sullivan, whose brother (Gene Barry) is eventually killed by Stanwyck's trigger-happy brother (John Ericson). A few action sequences keep the heavy plot moving with a finale that sees the town cleaned up and a reformed Stanwyck getting Sullivan.

Forceful as Stanwyck's performance is, at least one critic found

FORTY GUNS (1957). With John Ericson

her grim determination verging occasionally on caricature. Samuel Fuller, who has revealed that this was a role that Marilyn Monroe had once wanted very much to play, has expressed his admiration for his star's nerve and enterprise: "The stuntmen refused to do the scene where the Stanwyck character is dragged by a horse. They thought it was too dangerous. So Stanwyck said she'd do it. We did it the first time, and I said, 'I didn't like it. It was too far away from the camera truck. We're not getting what I want.' So we tried it again, and I didn't like it. She made no complaint. We tried it a third time, and it was just the way I wanted it. She was quite bruised."*

Forty Guns was Barbara Stanwyck's last feature film for four years. Later, when asked the reason for this unusual hiatus in a career known for its consecutive activity over the course of some twenty-eight years, she replied with characteristic frankness, "Because nobody asked me." And she added, "They don't normally write parts for women my age, because America is now a country of youth."

*Eric Sherman and Martin Rubin, *The Director's Event*, Atheneum, New York, 1970, pp. 149-50.

THE GRAND DAME: TELEVISION AND A NEW CAREER

In 1954, as a favor to her longtime friend Jack Benny, Barbara Stanwyck agreed to make her television debut with the veteran comedian in *Autolight,* a parody of the 1944 movie, *Gaslight.* They filmed it, but MGM, insisting that the story couldn't be spoofed without their permission, instituted a legal battle which went all the way to the Supreme Court. Eventually Benny had to purchase the rights in order to finally get his show on the air —five years later! For 1959 audiences, *Autolight* was well worth the wait. In the meantime, however, Stanwyck had managed to supplement a sporadic feature-film schedule with appearances on TV anthology series like "The Loretta Young Show," Dick Powell's "Zane Grey Theatre" and "Decision." And she campaigned, in vain, to get her own series—preferably a Western one.

In 1958 Stanwyck admitted having vetoed appearances on Ralph Edwards' "This Is Your Life" ("I would walk out") and Edward R. Murrow's "Person to Person" ("Who am I? Why should I be on a program like that? It's ridiculous"). Early the following year, it was announced that she would have her own NBC-TV anthology series, "The Barbara Stanwyck Show," in which she would alternate between starring and hostessing. Candid about her diminished drawing power as a Hollywood star, Stanwyck told columnist Marie Torre, "My plans have caused no great stir, and why should they? Friends and acquaintances have been saying to me, 'I see you're going into television—how nice.'" And she concluded, "How nice remains to be seen."

Indeed, a year and a half passed before the debut of "The Barbara Stanwyck Show" in September 1960. Of the thirty-six half-hour episodes filmed for this black-and-white series, Stanwyck starred in thirty-two, often opposite such actors as Lee Marvin, Joan Blondell and Ralph Bellamy. She worked hard to secure good scripts and experienced directors and technicians and, as Loretta Young had done, Stanwyck enjoyed a considerable variety of parts.

Later, recalling this series to columnist Kay Gardella, Stanwyck admitted, "I hated playing the role of hostess every week. I know Loretta Young loved it when she had her show on, but I couldn't stand it. I was lousy at it. I find I have to hide behind something. I can't just play myself."

In a January, 1961 *TV Guide* interview, she said: "Why did I

A WALK ON THE WILD SIDE (1962). As Jo Courtney

want to get into television? Simple. I wasn't working and I wanted to work. What else is there for me to do? I have no hobbies. I suppose that makes me an idiot, but there it is. You're supposed to paint or sculpt or something. I don't. I like to travel, but a woman can't travel alone. It's a bore. And it's a darned lonesome bore.

"People keep asking me what's the difference between doing pictures and TV, and I really can't see any difference. You're making film. The techniques are exactly the same. In television you work a little harder and a lot faster, that's all."

That spring Stanwyck sounded off in print with great agitation over the cancellation of her series, which had not been renewed for the 1961-62 season. "As I understand it from my producer Lou Edelman," she told Hollywood columnist Joe Hyams,

" 'they' want action shows and have a theory that women don't do action. The fact is, I'm the best action actress in the world. I can do horse drags and jump off buildings, and I have the scars to prove it."

As has happened several times to other newly cancelled series stars over the years, Barbara Stanwyck won a 1961 Emmy Award with "The Barbara Stanwyck Show," for "Outstanding Performance by an Actress in a Series."

By this time, however, she had accepted an offer from producer Charles K. Feldman at Columbia to return to feature-filmmaking in *A Walk on the Wild Side* (1962), ostensibly based on Nelson Algren's novel, but the result of much rewriting by five successive writers. As Bosley Crowther put it in *The New York Times*, "Edward Dmytryk's direction makes you wonder whether he read the script before he started shooting."

Bearing little resemblance to Algren's book, the film's languorous plot starts with Dove Linkhorn (Laurence Harvey) a Texas farmer of the 1930s, out searching for his long-lost love Hallie (Capucine), whom he eventually finds is the top attraction in a fancy New Orleans bordello called the Doll House, run by a no-nonsense lesbian named Jo

ROUSTABOUT (1964). With Elvis Presley

THE NIGHT WALKER (1965). As Irene Trent

Courtney (Stanwyck). In the meantime, Dove gets temporarily involved with a spirited young tramp (Jane Fonda) and a man-hungry Mexican widow (Anne Baxter), and in the melodramatic conclusion no one really comes out ahead, with Hallie shot dead and Jo taken away by the police.

Stanwyck's was a meaty supporting role in this confused and uneven melodrama, and although she received fifth billing, it caught the reader's eye—"and Barbara Stanwyck as Jo." There were those who criticized her acceptance of such a role, but she says, "It was a chance to get back to pictures and see what would happen," though she admits, "It could have been a damn good picture, but it just didn't work out."

The critics deplored *A Walk on the Wild Side,* and although it's trash, it is frequently entertaining trash, from Jane Fonda's lively gamine to Capucine's cool, Garboesque beauty to Anne Baxter's well-accented Latin flower ... and, of course, Stanwyck, who never flinches away from the suggestions of her interest in the girls, particularly Capucine, who has been sculpting a bust of her. When the atmosphere of the Doll House grows too heady, the dialogue waxes risible, as when Capucine tells Stanwyck, "I want to sit and drink with a man, not with you," and the latter retorts impatiently, "You're being perverse!"

Again, it was several years before another movie came Stanwyck's way. In the meantime, she returned to television, guest-starring several times on "Wagon Train," as well as "The Untouchables," "Rawhide" and "The Joey Bishop Show." Then came the unlikely casting that teamed her with no less than Elvis Presley in *Roustabout* (1964) for her old friend Hal Wallis at Paramount. It was a slight musical in a carnival setting, and she played a carnival owner who hires Elvis as a handyman and has his help in saving her from bankruptcy when he becomes the show's featured attraction. It was a role that Mae West had turned down, but Stanwyck ac-

With Ronald Reagan and Charlton Heston as she received the Screen Actors Guild Achievement Award (1966)

cepted it because she realized that appearing in a Presley film would introduce her to an entirely different kind of audience. And she has always enjoyed a challenge. *Variety*'s critic thought she was wasted, while Howard Thompson, in *The New York Times*, welcomed her return and applauded her "professional seasoning."

She then co-starred for the last time with Robert Taylor in a William Castle thriller for Universal, called *The Night Walker* (1965), which, to date, remains her last theatrical motion picture. It was a suspense story for which Castle had carefully approached both stars. Since each admired the other's work, the film came off with none of the problems that might have been expected with the professional teaming of a once-married couple. In fact, on-the-set photos showed them laughing and enjoying one another's company. As Stanwyck later told interviewer William Peper, "The first day on the set, everybody was peering at us. I don't know what they expected us to do. Maybe beat each other up. But we just made the picture."

THE HOUSE THAT WOULDN'T DIE (1970). With Michael Anderson, Jr.

Robert Bloch (of *Psycho* fame) wrote the screenplay of this original chiller about nightmares, both real and imagined. Stanwyck plays a blind man's wife whose recurrent dreams involve her with an attractive stranger (Lloyd Bochner), even after her husband is killed in a laboratory explosion. Taylor played the family lawyer, who helps Stanwyck get to the bottom of a series of weird events involving murder, a reappearance by her "dead" spouse—and a lot of terror for the film's heroine.

Because she, along with Castle and Taylor, owned a percentage of *The Night Walker*, Stanwyck then went off on an extensive personal appearance tour for Universal, during which she told interviewers about a Western-series pilot on which she was working and for which she had high hopes—"The Big Valley." When asked if she had any ideas of returning to the stage, Stanwyck replied, "Hell, no. No kind of money could drag me back to Broadway. Every now and then a theater producer sends me a script to consider. Merely touching the manila envelope, without opening it, makes me shake all over with fear of facing a live audience after all these years."

Fortunately for Stanwyck, "The Big Valley" found a sponsor, and in September 1965, it began a successful four-year run on the ABC network with its syndicated reruns continuing to be seen in many localities, as of this writing. With regular co-stars Richard Long, Peter Breck, Lee Majors and Linda Evans, she played the role of Victoria Barkley, widowed matriarch of a powerful ranching clan in California's San Joaquin Valley of the 1870s. As the actress told a reporter for the *New York Journal-American* in 1965, "I try to make Victoria Barkley as human as possible. She doesn't come waltzing down the stairs in calico to inquire as to the progress of the cattle. She's an old broad who combines elegance with guts." In a subsequent interview with Ezra Goodman,* she stressed that this was the first Western series featuring a woman, and added, "Some producers think women did nothing in those days except keep house and have children. But, if you read your history, they did a lot more than that. They were *in* cattle drives. They were *there*."

"As far as movies go," she told Goodman, "I don't think I'll be doing any while I'm busy with this series. Anyway, nobody's asked me. So there's nothing to worry about. I don't play romance anymore. That part is over. For my age bracket (58), I'm past the romantic thing and so you come to another age bracket, either good friend or

*Ezra Goodman, "My Name Is Barbara," *The New York Times*, October 17, 1965.

A TASTE OF EVIL (1971). As Miriam Jennings

mother, and they are mostly on the dull side and I'm not interested in doing them."

Of "The Big Valley's" 112 segments Stanwyck played in all but 7, with the size of her weekly segments varying as the show's writers continually shifted the emphasis from one to another of the Barkley clan. Virgil Vogel, who directed her in 45 episodes, and whom Stanwyck herself credits with knowing "as much about making Westerns as the old master, John Ford," says, "No physical action ever frightened Barbara. She has as much courage as any person I have ever known. She also had great confidence. I would give her all the protection possible. I checked each stunt carefully, but in her extreme dedication to her work she always gave a little more than she was instructed to. If I asked her to jump eight feet, she would do ten."*

In 1966, following "The Big Valley's" first season, Stanwyck won her second Emmy as "Outstanding Actress in a Dramatic Series," and in the next two years she won additional Emmy nominations for the series. But of all her citations, perhaps the one that moved Stanwyck the most was the Screen Actors Guild Award, presented to her in 1966 by Ronald Reagan, then California's governor-elect. As Reagan said in his speech: "The Screen Actors Guild Award is not presented just for long-time excellence on the screen. It should be called, perhaps, an above-and-beyond award, because it is given for outstanding achievement in fostering the finest ideals of the acting profession." In her emotional acceptance speech, Stanwyck said, "I love our profession very much. I love our people in it. And whatever little contribution I can make to the profession, or to anything, for that matter, I am very proud to do so."

Since filming "The Big Valley's"

*Ella Smith, *Starring Miss Barbara Stanwyck*, p. 294.

final segment, Barbara Stanwyck has made three 90-minute TV-movies: *The House that Wouldn't Die (1970)*, *A Taste of Evil* (1971), and *The Letters* (1973).

The first of these, filmed as *Ammie, Come Home* (the title of the Barbara Michaels novel on which Henry Farrell based his script), is a supernatural thriller about a woman (Stanwyck) who inherits an old Pennsylvania house reputed to be haunted. Cold, unexplained winds circulate inside it, and a ghostly presence succeeds in possessing her niece (Katherine—later Kitty—Winn), while neighbors Richard Egan and Michael Anderson, Jr. help solve the mystery with séances and investigations of attic and cellar. Some of this is rather exciting—and, at least the supernatural is not explained away as a hoax.

John Llewellyn Moxey, who directed both *The House That Wouldn't Die* and *A Taste of Evil* for ABC's "Movie of the Week" series, speaks highly of Stanwyck's professional discipline, her perfectionism, and her kindness to the less-experienced younger players. In *A Taste of Evil*, she plays a woman who is out to drive her daughter (Barbara Parkins) insane. Newly returned home from a mental hospital, the daughter is an easy target for a terror campaign waged by the mother in league with a servant (Arthur O'Connell), whom she forces to help her dispose of the girl. The motive for all this malevolence is an inheritance, which Stanwyck's late husband had deviously left to Parkins, whom he preferred to his wife.

Once the plot-reversals are revealed to the audience, Stanwyck's subtle but deadly character changes can be fully enjoyed for the skill with which she plays them. Written by British horror veteran Jimmy Sangster, *A Taste of Evil*, for all its implausibilities, is a highly entertaining chiller.

In the fall of 1971, Barbara Stanwyck was just beginning work on a CBS-TV movie called *Fitzgerald and Pride*, about a woman lawyer on a murder case, when she had to be rushed to the hospital for removal of a kidney. For a time, her life hung in the balance, and a long recuperation period followed. Her role in the movie, retitled *Heat of Anger*, was taken by Susan Hayward.

The Letters, Stanwyck's third "Movie of the Week" for ABC-TV, is an episodic multi-drama about three different groups of people whose lives are complicated and, in some instances, destroyed by a year-long delay in the delivery of a sack of mail, temporarily lost in a mountain plane crash. Stanwyck and Ida Lupino (who dominated another segment of the movie) were the only two of the movie's various stars singled out by the critics, who dubbed the whole enterprise "soap opera."

In her episode—the film's third and final one—Stanwyck plays the spiteful, dominating sister of nice Dina Merrill. Their privileged lives are temporarily brightened by the welcome intrusion of a handsome but fortune-hunting concert pianist (Leslie Nielsen), who soon shifts his attentions from Merrill to Stanwyck when he finds that *she* controls the family fortune. Stanwyck and Nielsen marry, but when she declines to back a concert tour that would separate them, he murders her. It's made to seem as though the lady took her own life—until the belated appearance of that letter informs Merrill of the truth, giving her a lifetime hold over Nielsen.

Under actor Gene Nelson's direction, Stanwyck's acting here is crisp and authoritative—and possessed of enough actor's energy to dissipate rumors that she had never fully recovered from her operation. Assigned to a 90-minute slot in March 1973, this complex drama, to accommodate the requisite number of commercials, could only run for 74 minutes of air-time. Consequently, because the original film ran some 25 minutes too long, three important scenes of the Stanwyck segment, had to be cut.

THE LETTERS (1973). With Dina Merrill and Leslie Nielsen

This explains the lack of development in an interesting character that seems to alter without sufficient time for transition or motivation.

Today, at sixty-seven, Barbara Stanwyck is still ready, willing and able to do what she enjoys most —act. Unfortunately, at this juncture, the motion picture medium—where she belongs—is still dominated by the on-screen *male* image, while women are all too frequently relegated to the background. Television has done better by older actresses, and that medium might predictably have more to offer Stanwyck, who once stated that she'd keep at her craft until she got so old they'd have to shoot her. In the meantime, for those who enjoy vigorous, assured, and down-to-earth acting, a lifetime of dedicated filmmaking is available to any television viewer tuning in a movie starring Barbara Stanwyck.

BIBLIOGRAPHY

American Film Institute, The. *The American Film Institute Catalog: Feature Films 1921-1930*. R.R. Bowker Co., New York, 1971.
Barbour, Alan G. *Humphrey Bogart*. Pyramid Publications, New York, 1973.
Baxter, John. *The Cinema of John Ford*. A. Zwemmer & A.S. Barnes, London and New York, 1971.
Bergman, Andrew. *James Cagney*. Pyramid Publications, New York, 1973.
Blackwell, Earl (ed.). *Celebrity Register*. Simon & Schuster, New York, 1973.
Bogdanovich, Peter. *Allan Dwan: The Last Pioneer*. Praeger Publishers, Inc., New York, 1971.
———. *Fritz Lang in America*. Praeger Publishers, Inc., New York, 1967.
———. *John Ford*. A. Zwemmer & A.S. Barnes, London and New York, 1967.
Canham, Kingsley. *The Hollywood Professionals, Volume 2* (Lewis Milestone chapter). The Tantivy Press & A.S. Barnes, New York and London, 1974.
Capra, Frank. *The Name Above the Title*. The Macmillan Co., New York, 1971.
Chierichetti, David. *Hollywood Director: Mitchell Leisen*. Curtis Books, New York, 1973.
Conway, Michael and Mark Ricci. *The Films of Marilyn Monroe*. The Citadel Press, New York, 1964.
Dickens, Homer. *The Films of Gary Cooper*. The Citadel Press, New York, 1970.
———. *The Films of James Cagney*. The Citadel Press, Secaucus, New Jersey, 1972.
Essoe, Gabe. *The Films of Clark Gable*. The Citadel Press, New York, 1970.
Garnham, Nicholas. *Samuel Fuller*. The Viking Press, New York, 1971.
Greene, Graham. *Graham Greene on Film*. Simon & Schuster, New York, 1972.
Griffith, Richard. *Frank Capra*. The British Film Institute, London, 1949.
Halliday, Jon. *Sirk on Sirk*. The Viking Press, New York, 1972.
Hardy, Phil. *Samuel Fuller*. Praeger Publishers, Inc., New York, 1970.
Higham, Charles and Joel Greenberg. *The Celluloid Muse*. Henry Regnery Co., Chicago, 1969.
———. *Hollywood in the Forties*. A.S. Barnes, New York, 1968.
Jensen, Paul M. *The Cinema of Fritz Lang*. A.S. Barnes, New York, 1969.
Jordan, René. *Gary Cooper*. Pyramid Publications, New York, 1974.

Mantle, Burns. *The Best Plays of 1919-1920, —1923-24, —1924-1925, —1926-1927, —1927-1928, —1928-1929, —1932-1933, —1937-1938, —1941-1942, —1943-1944, —1944-1945, —1946-1947.* Dodd, Mead & Co., New York.

McCarty, Clifford. *Bogey: The Films of Humphrey Bogart.* The Citadel Press, New York, 1965.

Milne, Tom. *Mamoulian.* Indiana University Press, Bloomington, 1969.

Parish, James Robert. *Actors' Television Credits: 1950-1972.* The Scarecrow Press, Metuchen, New Jersey, 1973.

Quirk, Lawrence J. *The Films of William Holden.* The Citadel Press, Secaucus, New Jersey, 1973.

Ringgold, Gene and Bodeen, DeWitt. *The Films of Cecil B. DeMille.* The Citadel Press, New York, 1969.

Ringgold, Gene. *Barbara Stanwyck.* Article in *Films in Review*, December 1963.

Rosen, Marjorie. *Popcorn Venus.* Coward, McCann & Geoghegan, New York, 1973.

Sennett, Ted. *Lunatics and Lovers.* Arlington House, New Rochelle, 1974.

———. *Warner Brothers Presents.* Arlington House, New Rochelle, 1971.

Sherman, Eric and Martin Rubin. *The Director's Event.* Atheneum, New York, 1970.

Smith, Ella. *Starring Miss Barbara Stanwyck.* Crown Publishers, New York, 1974.

Springer, John. *The Fondas.* The Citadel Press, New York, 1970.

Thomas, Bob. *King Cohn.* G.P. Putnam's Sons, New York, 1967.

Thomas, Tony, Rudy Behlmer and Clifford McCarty. *The Films of Errol Flynn.* The Citadel Press, New York, 1969.

Thomas, Tony. *The Films of Kirk Douglas.* The Citadel Press, Secaucus, New Jersey, 1972.

Ursini, James. *Preston Sturges.* Curtis Books, New York, 1973.

Wayne, Jane Ellen. *The Life of Robert Taylor.* Warner Paperback Library, New York, 1973.

THE FILMS OF BARBARA STANWYCK

The director's name follows the release date. A (c) following the release date indicates that the film was in color. Sp indicates Screenplay and b/o indicates based/on.

1. BROADWAY NIGHTS. First National, 1927. *Joseph C. Boyle.* Sp: Forrest Halsey, b/o story by Norman Houston. Cast: Lois Wilson, Sam Hardy, Louis John Bartels, Philip Strange, Bunny Weldon.

2. THE LOCKED DOOR. United Artists, 1929. *George Fitzmaurice.* Sp: C. Gardner Sullivan and George Scarborough, b/o play by Channing Pollock. Cast: Rod La Rocque, William Boyd, Betty Bronson, Harry Stubbs, Harry Mestayer, Mack Swain, ZaSu Pitts. Originally filmed in 1921 as *The Sign on the Door.*

3. MEXICALI ROSE. Columbia, 1929. *Erle C. Kenton.* Sp: Gladys Lehman and Norman Houston. Cast: Sam Hardy, William Janney, Louis Natheaux, Arthur Rankin, Harry Vejar, Louis King.

4. LADIES OF LEISURE. Columbia, 1930. *Frank Capra.* Sp: Jo Swerling, b/o play by Milton Herbert Gropper. Cast: Ralph Graves, Lowell Sherman, Marie Prevost, Nance O'Neil, George Fawcett, Johnnie Walker. Remade in 1937 as *Women of Glamour.*

5. ILLICIT. Warners, 1931. *Archie Mayo.* Sp: Harvey Thew, b/o play by Edith Fitzgerald and Robert Riskin. Cast: James Rennie, Ricardo Cortez, Natalie Moorhead, Charles Butterworth, Joan Blondell, Claude Gillingwater.

6. TEN CENTS A DANCE. Columbia, 1931. *Lionel Barrymore.* Sp: Jo Swerling. Cast: Ricardo Cortez, Monroe Owsley, Sally Blane, Martha Sleeper, Blanche Frederici, David Newell.

7. NIGHT NURSE. Warners, 1931. *William A. Wellman.* Sp: Oliver H.P. Garrett, b/o novel by Dora Macy. Cast: Ben Lyon, Joan Blondell, Clark Gable, Blanche Frederici, Charlotte Merriam, Charles Winninger, Edward Nugent, Vera Lewis, Ralf Harolde.

8. THE MIRACLE WOMAN. Columbia, 1931. *Frank Capra*. Sp: Jo Swerling, b/o play by John Meehan and Robert Riskin. Cast: David Manners, Sam Hardy, Beryl Mercer, Russell Hopton.

9. FORBIDDEN. Columbia, 1932. *Frank Capra*. Sp: Jo Swerling, b/o story by Capra. Cast: Adolphe Menjou, Ralph Bellamy, Dorothy Peterson, Charlotte V. Henry, Thomas Jefferson, Halliwell Hobbes.

10. SHOPWORN. Columbia, 1932. *Nicholas Grinde*. Sp: Jo Swerling and Robert Riskin, b/o story by Sarah Y. Mason. Cast: Regis Toomey, ZaSu Pitts, Lucien Littlefield, Clara Blandick, Oscar Apfel.

11. SO BIG. Warners, 1932. *William A. Wellman*. Sp: J. Grubb Alexander and Robert Lord, b/o novel by Edna Ferber. Cast: George Brent, Dickie Moore, Guy Kibbee, Bette Davis, Mae Madison, Hardie Albright, Robert Warwick, Alan Hale, Arthur Stone, Dorothy Peterson, Dawn O'Day (Anne Shirley), Elizabeth Patterson. Previously filmed in 1924 and remade in 1953.

12. THE PURCHASE PRICE. Warners, 1932. *William A. Wellman*. Sp: Robert Lord, b/o story by Arthur Stringer. Cast: George Brent, Lyle Talbot, Hardie Albright, David Landau, Murray Kinnell, Leila Bennett, Matt McHugh, Dawn O'Day (Anne Shirley), Mae Busch.

13. THE BITTER TEA OF GENERAL YEN. Columbia, 1933. *Frank Capra*. Sp: Edward Paramore, b/o novel by Grace Zaring Stone. Cast: Nils Asther, Toshia Mori, Walter Connolly, Gavin Gordon, Lucien Littlefield, Richard Loo, Helen Jerome Eddy, Clara Blandick.

14. LADIES THEY TALK ABOUT. Warners, 1933. *Howard Bretherton* and *William Keighley*. Sp: Sidney Sutherland and Brown Holmes, b/o play by Dorothy Mackaye and Carlton Miles. Cast: Preston Foster, Lyle Talbot, Dorothy Burgess, Lillian Roth, Maude Eburne, Harold Huber, Ruth Donnelly, Robert Warwick, Cecil Cunningham, Helen Ware. Remade in 1942 as *Lady Gangster*.

15. BABY FACE. Warners, 1933. *Alfred E. Green*. Sp: Gene Markey and Kathryn Scola, b/o story by Mark Canfield. Cast: George Brent, Donald Cook, Alphonse Ethier, Henry Kolker, Robert Barrat, Theresa Harris, Douglass Dumbrille, Arthur Hohl, Margaret Lindsay, Nat Pendleton, John Wayne, Toby Wing, Renee Whitney.

16. EVER IN MY HEART. Warners, 1933. *Archie Mayo*. Sp: Bertram Milhauser, b/o story by Milhauser and Beulah Marie Dix. Cast: Otto Kruger, Ralph Bellamy, Ruth Donnelly, Frank Albertson, Laura Hope Crews, Frank Reicher, Clara Blandick, Nella Walker, George Cooper, Wallis Clark, Florence Roberts, Henry O'Neill, Ronnie Crosby, Bess Flowers, Willard Robertson, Elizabeth Patterson.

17. GAMBLING LADY. Warners, 1934. *Archie Mayo.* Sp: Ralph Block and Doris Malloy, b/o story by Malloy. Cast: Joel McCrea, Pat O'Brien, Claire Dodd, C. Aubrey Smith, Robert Barrat, Arthur Vinton, Phillip Reed, Philip Faversham, Ferdinand Gottschalk, Arthur Treacher, Robert Elliott, Willard Robertson.

18. A LOST LADY. First National, 1934. *Alfred E. Green.* Sp: Gene Markey and Kathryn Scola, b/o novel by Willa Cather. Cast: Frank Morgan, Ricardo Cortez, Lyle Talbot, Phillip Reed, Hobart Cavanaugh, Henry Kolker, Rafaela Ottiano, Samuel Hinds, Edward McWade. Previously filmed in 1924.

19. THE SECRET BRIDE. Warners, 1935. *William Dieterle.* Sp: Tom Buckingham, F. Hugh Herbert and Mary McCall Jr., b/o play by Leonard Ide. Cast: Warren William, Glenda Farrell, Grant Mitchell, Arthur Byron, Henry O'Neill, Douglass Dumbrille, Willard Robertson.

20. THE WOMAN IN RED. First National, 1935. *Robert Florey.* Sp: Mary McCall Jr. and Peter Milne, b/o novel by Wallace Irwin. Cast: Gene Raymond, Genevieve Tobin, John Eldredge, Phillip Reed, Dorothy Tree, Russell Hicks, Nella Walker, Doris Lloyd, Claude Gillingwater, Arthur Treacher, Hale Hamilton.

21. RED SALUTE (Rereleased as RUNAWAY DAUGHTER). Reliance/United Artists, 1935. *Sidney Lanfield.* Sp: Humphrey Pearson and Manuel Seff, b/o story by Pearson. Cast: Robert Young, Hardie Albright, Cliff Edwards, Ruth Donnelly, Gordon Jones, Paul Stanton, Nella Walker, Purnell Pratt, Henry Kolker, Arthur Vinton.

22. ANNIE OAKLEY. RKO, 1935. *George Stevens.* Sp: Joel Sayre and John Twist, b/o story by Joseph A. Fields and Ewart Adamson. Cast: Preston Foster, Melvyn Douglas, Moroni Olsen, Pert Kelton, Andy Clyde, Margaret Armstrong, Chief Thunderbird, Delmar Watson.

23. A MESSAGE TO GARCIA. 20th Century-Fox, 1936. *George Marshall.* Sp: W.P. Lipscomb and Gene Fowler, b/o essay by Elbert Hubbard and book by Andrew S. Rowan. Cast: Wallace Beery, John Boles, Herbert Mundin, Mona Barrie, Enrique Acosta, Martin Garralaga, Juan Torena, Blanca Vischer, Rita Cansino (Hayworth).

24. THE BRIDE WALKS OUT. RKO, 1936. *Leigh Jason.* Sp: P.J. Wolfson and Philip G. Epstein, b/o story by Howard Emmett Rogers. Cast: Gene Raymond, Robert Young, Ned Sparks, Helen Broderick, Willie Best, Robert Warwick, Billy Gilbert, Hattie McDaniel, Irving Bacon.

25. HIS BROTHER'S WIFE. MGM, 1936. *W.S. Van Dyke.* Sp: Leon Gordon and John Meehan, b/o story by George Auerbach. Cast: Robert Taylor, Jean Hersholt, Joseph Calleia, John Eldredge, Samuel S. Hinds, Leonard Mudie, Jed Prouty, Pedro De Cordoba.

26. BANJO ON MY KNEE. 20th Century-Fox, 1936. *John Cromwell.* Sp: Nunnally Johnson, b/o novel by Harry Hamilton. Cast: Joel McCrea, Walter Brennan, Buddy Ebsen, Helen Westley, Walter Catlett, Anthony (later Tony) Martin, Katherine DeMille, Victor Kilian, Minna Gombell, Spencer Charters, the Hall Johnson Choir.

27. THE PLOUGH AND THE STARS. RKO, 1937. *John Ford.* Sp: Dudley Nichols, b/o play by Sean O'Casey. Cast: Preston Foster, Barry Fitzgerald, Denis O'Dea, Eileen Crowe, F.J. McCormick, Arthur Shields, Una O'Connor, Moroni Olsen, Bonita Granville, J.M. Kerrigan, Erin O'Brien-Moore, Mary Gordon, Doris Lloyd.

28. INTERNES CAN'T TAKE MONEY. Paramount, 1937. *Alfred Santell.* Sp: Rian James and Theodore Reeves, b/o story by Max Brand. Cast: Joel McCrea, Lloyd Nolan, Stanley Ridges, Lee Bowman, Barry Macollum, Irving Bacon, Gaylord Pendleton, Pierre Watkin, Priscilla Lawson, Fay Holden, Sarah Padden, James Bush.

29. THIS IS MY AFFAIR. 20th Century-Fox, 1937. *William A. Seiter.* Sp: Allen Rivkin and Lamar Trotti. Cast: Robert Taylor, Victor McLaglen, Brian Donlevy, Sidney Blackmer, John Carradine, Alan Dinehart, Douglas Fowley, Robert McWade, Frank Conroy, Sig Rumann.

30. STELLA DALLAS. Samuel Goldwyn/United Artists, 1937. *King Vidor.* Sp: Harry Wagstaff Gribble and Gertrude Purcell, b/o novel by Olive Higgins Prouty. Cast: John Boles, Anne Shirley, Barbara O'Neil, Alan Hale, Marjorie Main, Ann Shoemaker, Tim Holt, Nella Walker, Jimmy Butler, Dickie Jones, Lillian Yarbo. Previously filmed in 1925.

31. BREAKFAST FOR TWO. RKO, 1937. *Alfred Santell.* Sp: Charles Kaufman, Paul Yawitz and Viola Brothers Shore, b/o story by David Garth. Cast: Herbert Marshall, Glenda Farrell, Eric Blore, Frank M. Thomas, Donald Meek, Pierre Watkin, Etienne Girardot.

32. ALWAYS GOODBYE. 20th Century-Fox, 1938. *Sidney Lanfield.* Sp: Kathryn Scola and Edith Skouras, b/o story by Gilbert Emery and Douglas Doty. Cast: Herbert Marshall, Ian Hunter, Cesar Romero, Lynn Bari, Binnie Barnes, Johnny Russell, Mary Forbes, Albert Conti, Franklin Pangborn, Marcelle Corday. A remake of *Gallant Lady* (1934).

33. THE MAD MISS MANTON. RKO, 1938. *Leigh Jason.* Sp: Philip G. Epstein, b/o story by Wilson Collison. Cast: Henry Fonda, Sam Levene, Frances Mercer, Stanley Ridges, Whitney Bourne, Vicki Lester, Ann Evers, Hattie McDaniel, James Burke, Penny Singleton, Paul Guilfoyle, Grady Sutton, John Qualen, Miles Mander.

34. UNION PACIFIC. Paramount, 1939. *Cecil B. DeMille.* Sp: Walter DeLeon, C. Gardner Sullivan and Jesse Lasky Jr., b/o story by Ernest Haycox. Cast: Joel McCrea, Robert Preston, Akim Tamiroff, Lynne Overman, Brian Donlevy, Anthony Quinn, Evelyn Keyes, Stanley Ridges, Regis Toomey, Syd Saylor, J.M. Kerrigan, William Haade, Fuzzy Knight, Francis MacDonald, Henry Kolker, Julia Faye.

35. GOLDEN BOY. Columbia, 1939. *Rouben Mamoulian.* Sp: Lewis Meltzer, Daniel Taradash, Sarah Y. Mason and Victor Heerman, b/o play by Clifford Odets. Cast: Adolphe Menjou, William Holden, Lee J. Cobb, Joseph Calleia, Sam Levene, Edward S. Brophy, Beatrice Blinn.

36. REMEMBER THE NIGHT. Paramount, 1940. *Mitchell Leisen.* Sp: Preston Sturges. Cast: Fred MacMurray, Beulah Bondi, Elizabeth Patterson, Willard Robertson, Sterling Holloway, Charles Waldron, Paul Guilfoyle, Charles Arnt, John Wray, Georgia Caine, Tom Kennedy.

37. THE LADY EVE. Paramount, 1941. *Preston Sturges.* Sp: Preston Sturges, b/o story by Monckton Hoffe. Cast: Henry Fonda, Charles Coburn, Eugene Pallette, William Demarest, Eric Blore, Melville Cooper, Martha O'Driscoll, Janet Beecher, Robert Grieg. Remade in 1956 as *The Birds and the Bees*.

38. MEET JOHN DOE. Warners, 1941. *Frank Capra.* Sp: Robert Riskin, b/o story by Richard Connell and Robert Presnell. Cast: Gary Cooper, Edward Arnold, Walter Brennan, Spring Byington, James Gleason, Gene Lockhart, Rod La Rocque, Irving Bacon, Regis Toomey, J. Farrell MacDonald, Warren Hymer, Andrew Tombes, Pierre Watkin, Ann Doran.

39. YOU BELONG TO ME. Columbia, 1941. *Wesley Ruggles.* Sp: Claude Binyon, b/o story by Dalton Trumbo. Cast: Henry Fonda, Edgar Buchanan, Roger Clark, Ruth Donnelly, Melville Cooper, Ralph Peters, Maude Eburne, Renie Riano, Mary Treen, Gordon Jones. Remade in 1950 as *Emergency Wedding*.

40. BALL OF FIRE. RKO, 1941. *Howard Hawks.* Sp: Charles Brackett and Billy Wilder, b/o story by Wilder and Thomas Monroe. Cast: Gary Cooper, Oscar Homolka, Henry Travers, S.Z. Sakall, Tully Marshall, Leonid Kinskey, Richard Haydn, Aubrey Mather, Allen Jenkins, Dana Andrews, Dan Duryea, Ralph Peters, Kathleen Howard, Charles Arnt. Remade in 1948 as *A Song is Born*.

41. THE GREAT MAN'S LADY. Paramount, 1942. *William A. Wellman.* Sp: W.L. River, b/o original story by Adela Rogers St. Johns and Seena Owen, from short story by Viña Delmar. Cast: Joel McCrea, Brian Donlevy, Katharine (Later "K.T.") Stevens, Thurston Hall, Lloyd Corrigan, Etta McDaniel, Frank M. Thomas, William B. Davidson.

42. THE GAY SISTERS. Warners, 1942. *Irving Rapper*. Sp: Lenore Coffee, b/o novel by Stephen Longstreet. Cast: George Brent, Geraldine Fitzgerald, Donald Crisp, Gig Young, Nancy Coleman, Gene Lockhart, Larry Simms, Donald Woods, Grant Mitchell, Anne Revere, Helene Thimig.

43. LADY OF BURLESQUE. Hunt Stromberg/United Artists, 1943. *William A. Wellman*. Sp: James Gunn, b/o novel by Gypsy Rose Lee. Cast: Michael O'Shea, J. Edward Bromberg, Iris Adrian, Gloria Dickson, Victoria Faust, Stephanie Bachelor, Charles Dingle, Marion Martin, Eddie Gordon, Frank Fenton, Pinky Lee, Frank Conroy, Janis Carter.

44. FLESH AND FANTASY. Universal, 1943. *Julien Duvivier*. Sp: Ernest Pascal, Samuel Hoffenstein and Ellis St. Joseph, b/o stories by St. Joseph, Oscar Wilde and Laslo Vadnay. Cast: Edward G. Robinson, Charles Boyer, Betty Field, Robert Cummings, Thomas Mitchell, Charles Winninger, Anna Lee, Dame May Whitty, C. Aubrey Smith, Robert Benchley.

45. DOUBLE INDEMNITY. Paramount, 1944. *Billy Wilder*. Sp: Billy Wilder and Raymond Chandler, b/o novel by James M. Cain. Cast: Fred MacMurray, Edward G. Robinson, Porter Hall, Jean Heather, Tom Powers, Byron Barr, Richard Gaines, Fortunio Bonanova.

46. HOLLYWOOD CANTEEN. Warners, 1944. *Delmer Daves*. Sp: Delmer Daves. Cast: Joan Leslie, Robert Hutton, Dane Clark, Janis Paige. With many guest stars.

47. CHRISTMAS IN CONNECTICUT. Warners, 1945. *Peter Godfrey*. Sp: Lionel Houser and Adele Comandini, b/o story by Aileen Hamilton. Cast: Dennis Morgan, Sydney Greenstreet, Reginald Gardiner, S.Z. Sakall, Robert Shayne, Una O'Connor, Frank Jenks, Joyce Compton.

48. MY REPUTATION. Warners, 1946. *Curtis Bernhardt*. Sp: Catherine Turney, b/o novel by Clare Jaynes. Cast: George Brent, Warner Anderson, Lucile Watson, John Ridgely, Eve Arden, Jerome Cowan, Esther Dale, Scotty Beckett, Bobby Cooper, Leona Maricle, Cecil Cunningham, Janis Wilson, Ann E. Todd, Mary Servoss.

49. THE BRIDE WORE BOOTS. Paramount, 1946. *Irving Pichel*. Sp: Dwight Mitchell Wiley, b/o story by Wiley and play by Harry Segall. Cast: Robert Cummings, Diana Lynn, Patric Knowles, Peggy Wood, Robert Benchley, Willie Best, Natalie Wood, Gregory Muradian.

50. THE STRANGE LOVE OF MARTHA IVERS. Paramount, 1946. *Lewis Milestone*. Sp: Robert Rossen, b/o story by Jack Patrick. Cast: Van Heflin, Lizabeth Scott, Kirk Douglas, Judith Anderson, Roman Bohnen, Darryl Hickman, Janis Wilson, Ann Doran, Frank Orth, James Flavin.

51. CALIFORNIA. Paramount, 1947. (c) *John Farrow*. Sp: Frank Butler and Theodore Strauss, b/o story by Boris Ingster. Cast: Ray Milland, Barry Fitzgerald, George Coulouris, Albert Dekker, Anthony Quinn, Frank Faylen, Gavin Muir, James Burke, Eduardo Ciannelli, Roman Bohnen, Argentina Brunetti, Howard Freeman, Julia Faye.

52. THE TWO MRS. CARROLLS. Warners, 1947. *Peter Godfrey*. Sp: Thomas Job, b/o play by Martin Vale. Cast: Humphrey Bogart, Alexis Smith, Nigel Bruce, Isobel Elsom, Pat O'Moore, Ann Carter, Anita Bolster.

53. THE OTHER LOVE. Enterprise/United Artists, 1947. *Andre de Toth*. Sp: Harry Brown and Ladislas Fodor, b/o short story by Erich Maria Remarque. Cast: David Niven, Richard Conte, Gilbert Roland, Joan Lorring, Lenore Aubert, Maria Palmer, Natalie Schafer.

54. CRY WOLF. Warners, 1947. *Peter Godfrey*. Sp: Catherine Turney, b/o novel by Marjorie Carleton. Cast: Errol Flynn, Geraldine Brooks, Richard Basehart, Jerome Cowan, John Ridgely, Patricia White, Rory Mallinson, Helene Thimig, Paul Stanton.

55. VARIETY GIRL. Paramount, 1947. *George Marshall*. Sp: Edmund Hartmann, Frank Tashlin, Robert Welch and Monte Brice. Cast: Mary Hatcher, Olga San Juan, DeForest Kelley, William Demarest, Frank Faylen, Frank Ferguson, Glenn Tryon. With many guest stars.

56. B.F.'S DAUGHTER. MGM, 1948. *Robert Z. Leonard*. Sp: Luther Davis, b/o novel by J.P. Marquand. Cast: Van Heflin, Charles Coburn, Richard Hart, Keenan Wynn, Margaret Lindsay, Spring Byington, Marshall Thompson, Barbara Laage, Thomas E. Breen.

57. SORRY, WRONG NUMBER. Paramount, 1948. *Anatole Litvak*. Sp: Lucille Fletcher, b/o her radio play. Cast: Burt Lancaster, Ann Richards, Wendell Corey, Harold Vermilyea, Ed Begley, Leif Erickson, William Conrad, John Bromfield, Jimmy Hunt, Kristine Miller.

58. THE LADY GAMBLES. Universal, 1949. *Michael Gordon*. Sp: Roy Huggins, b/o story by Lewis Meltzer and Oscar Saul and adaptation by Halsted Welles. Cast: Robert Preston, Stephen McNally, Edith Barrett, John Hoyt, Phil Van Zandt, Leif Erickson, Curt Conway, Nana Bryant, Anthony (Tony) Curtis.

59. EAST SIDE, WEST SIDE. MGM, 1949. *Mervyn LeRoy*. Sp: Isobel Lennart, b/o novel by Marcia Davenport. Cast: James Mason, Van Heflin, Ava Gardner, Cyd Charisse, Nancy Davis, Gale Sondergaard, William Conrad, Douglas Kennedy, Beverly Michaels, William Frawley.

60. THELMA JORDAN (THE FILE ON THELMA JORDAN). Paramount, 1950. *Robert Siodmak*. Sp: Ketti Frings, b/o story by Marty Holland. Cast: Wendell Corey, Paul Kelly, Joan Tetzel, Stanley Ridges, Richard Rober, Minor Watson, Barry Kelley, Laura Elliot, Basil Ruysdael.

61. NO MAN OF HER OWN. Paramount, 1950. *Mitchell Leisen*. Sp: Sally Benson and Catherine Turney, b/o novel by William Irish. Cast: John Lund, Jane Cowl, Phyllis Thaxter, Lyle Bettger, Henry O'Neill, Richard Denning, Carole Mathews, Harry Antrim, Catherine Craig, Esther Dale, Milburn Stone, Griff Barnett, Georgia Backus.

62. THE FURIES. Paramount, 1950. *Anthony Mann*. Sp: Charles Schnee, b/o novel by Niven Busch. Cast: Wendell Corey, Walter Huston, Judith Anderson, Gilbert Roland, Thomas Gomez, Beulah Bondi, Albert Dekker, John Bromfield, Wallace Ford, Blanche Yurka.

63. TO PLEASE A LADY. MGM, 1950. *Clarence Brown*. Sp: Barré Lyndon and Marge Decker. Cast: Clark Gable, Adolphe Menjou, Will Geer, Roland Winters, William C. McGaw, Lela Bliss, Emory Parnell.

64. THE MAN WITH A CLOAK. MGM, 1951. *Fletcher Markle*. Sp: Frank Fenton, b/o story by John Dickson Carr. Cast: Joseph Cotten, Louis Calhern, Leslie Caron, Joe De Santis, Jim Backus, Margaret Wycherly, Richard Hale, Nicholas Joy, Roy Roberts.

65. CLASH BY NIGHT. RKO, 1952. *Fritz Lang*. Sp: Alfred Hayes, b/o play by Clifford Odets. Cast: Paul Douglas, Robert Ryan, Marilyn Monroe, J. Carrol Naish, Keith Andes, Silvio Minciotti.

66. JEOPARDY. MGM, 1953. *John Sturges*. Sp: Mel Dinelli, b/o story by Maurice Zimm. Cast: Barry Sullivan, Ralph Meeker, Lee Aaker.

67. TITANIC. 20th Century-Fox, 1953. *Jean Negulesco*. Sp: Charles Brackett, Walter Reisch and Richard Breen. Cast: Clifton Webb, Robert Wagner, Audrey Dalton, Thelma Ritter, Brian Aherne, Richard Basehart, Allyn Joslyn, Edmund Purdom, Mae Marsh.

68. ALL I DESIRE. Universal-International, 1953. *Douglas Sirk*. Sp: James Gunn and Robert Blees, b/o novel by Carol Ryrie Brink. Cast: Richard Carlson, Lyle Bettger, Marcia Henderson, Lori Nelson, Maureen O'Sullivan, Richard Long, Billy Gray, Lotte Stein.

69. THE MOONLIGHTER. Warners, 1953. *Roy Rowland*. Sp: Niven Busch. Cast: Fred MacMurray, Ward Bond, William Ching, John Dierkes, Morris Ankrum, Jack Elam, Charles Halton, Norman Leavitt.

70. BLOWING WILD. Warners, 1953. *Hugo Fregonese*. Sp: Philip Yordan. Cast: Gary Cooper, Ruth Roman, Anthony Quinn, Ward Bond, Ian MacDonald, Richard Karlan.

71. WITNESS TO MURDER. Chester Erskine/United Artists, 1954. *Roy Rowland*. Sp: Chester Erskine. Cast: George Sanders, Gary Merrill, Jesse White, Harry Shannon, Claire Carleton, Lewis Martin, Dick Elliott, Harry Tyler, Juanita Moore, Adeline De Walt Reynolds.

72. EXECUTIVE SUITE. MGM, 1954. *Robert Wise*. Sp: Ernest Lehman, b/o novel by Cameron Hawley. Cast: William Holden, June Allyson, Fredric March, Walter Pidgeon, Shelley Winters, Paul Douglas, Louis Calhern, Nina Foch, Tim Considine, William Phipps, Virginia Brissac.

73. CATTLE QUEEN OF MONTANA. RKO, 1955. (c) *Allan Dwan*. Sp: Howard Estabrook and Robert Blees, b/o story by Thomas Blackburn. Cast: Ronald Reagan, Gene Evans, Lance Fuller, Anthony Caruso, Jack Elam, Yvette Dugay, Morris Ankrum, Myron Healey, Chubby Johnson.

74. THE VIOLENT MEN. Columbia, 1955. (c) *Rudolph Maté*. Sp: Harry Kleiner, b/o novel by Donald Hamilton. Cast: Glenn Ford, Edward G. Robinson, Dianne Foster, Brian Keith, May Wynn, Warner Anderson, Basil Ruysdael, Lita Milan, Richard Jaeckel, Jack Kelly.

75. ESCAPE TO BURMA. RKO, 1955 (c) *Allan Dwan*. Sp: Talbot Jennings and Hobart Donavan, b/o story by Kenneth Perkins. Cast: Robert Ryan, David Farrar, Murvyn Vye, Lisa Montell, Robert Warwick, Reginald Denny, Peter Coe, Alex Montoya.

76. THERE'S ALWAYS TOMORROW. Universal, 1956. *Douglas Sirk*. Sp: Bernard C. Schoenfeld, b/o story by Ursula Parrott. Cast: Fred MacMurray, Joan Bennett, Pat Crowley, William Reynolds, Gigi Perreau, Judy Nugent, Jane Darwell. Previously filmed in 1934.

77. THE MAVERICK QUEEN. Republic, 1956. (c) *Joseph Kane*. Sp: Kenneth Gamet and DeVallon Scott, b/o novel by Zane Grey. Cast: Barry Sullivan, Scott Brady, Mary Murphy, Wallace Ford, Howard Petrie, Jim Davis, Emile Meyer, Walter Sande, Taylor Holmes.

78. THESE WILDER YEARS. MGM, 1956. *Roy Rowland*. Sp: Frank Fenton, b/o story by Ralph Wheelwright. Cast: James Cagney, Walter Pidgeon, Betty Lou Keim, Don Dubbins, Edward Andrews, Basil Ruysdael, Grandon Rhodes, Dean Jones.

79. CRIME OF PASSION. Bob Goldstein/United Artists, 1957. *Gerd Oswald*. Sp: Jo Eisinger. Cast: Sterling Hayden, Raymond Burr, Fay Wray, Royal Dano, Virginia Grey, Dennis Cross, Jay Adler.

80. TROOPER HOOK. United Artists, 1957. *Charles Marquis Warren*. Sp: Warren, David Victor and Herbert Little Jr., b/o story by Jack Schaefer. Cast: Joel McCrea, Earl Holliman, Edward Andrews, John Dehner, Susan Kohner, Royal Dano, Terry Lawrence, Celia Lovsky, Rodolfo Acosta.

81. FORTY GUNS. 20th Century-Fox, 1957. *Samuel Fuller*. Sp: Fuller. Cast: Barry Sullivan, Dean Jagger, John Ericson, Gene Barry, Robert Dix, Jidge Carroll, Paul Dubov, Ziva Rodann, Eve Brent.

82. A WALK ON THE WILD SIDE. Columbia, 1962. *Edward Dmytryk*. Sp: John Fante and Edmund Morris, b/o novel by Nelson Algren. Cast: Laurence Harvey, Capucine, Jane Fonda, Anne Baxter, Joanna Moore, Richard Rust, Karl Swenson, Donald Barry, Juanita Moore, John Anderson, Ken Lynch, Todd Armstrong, Lillian Bronson.

83. ROUSTABOUT. Paramount, 1964. (c) *John Rich*. Sp: Anthony Lawrence and Allan Weiss, b/o story by Weiss. Cast: Elvis Presley, Joan Freeman, Leif Erickson, Sue Ane Langdon, Pat Buttram, Joan Staley, Dabbs Greer, Steve Brodie, Jack Albertson, Jane Dulo.

84. THE NIGHT WALKER. Universal, 1965. *William Castle*. Sp: Robert Bloch. Cast: Robert Taylor, Judith Meredith, Hayden Rorke, Rochelle Hudson, Marjorie Bennett, Jess Barker, Lloyd Bochner.

85. THE HOUSE THAT WOULDN'T DIE. ABC-TV, 1970. (c) *John Llewellyn Moxey*. Teleplay: Henry Farrell, b/o novel by Barbara Michaels. Cast: Richard Egan, Michael Anderson Jr., Katherine (Kitty) Winn, Doreen Lang, Mabel Albertson.

86. A TASTE OF EVIL. ABC-TV, 1971. (c) *John Llewellyn Moxey*. Teleplay: Jimmy Sangster. Cast: Barbara Parkins, Roddy McDowall, William Windom, Arthur O'Connell, Bing Russell, Dawn Frame.

87. THE LETTERS. ABC-TV, 1973. (c) *Gene Nelson*. Teleplay (Stanwyck episode): Ellis Marcus and Hal Sitowitz, b/o story by Marcus. Cast: Story I—John Forsythe, Jane Powell, Lesley Warren; Story II—Ida Lupino, Pamela Franklin, Ben Murphy; Story III—Barbara Stanwyck, Leslie Nielsen, Dina Merrill.

INDEX

Aaker, Lee, 112
Abbey Theatre, 51
Acosta, Rodolfo, 125
Adler, Luther, 66
Adrian, Iris, 81
Aherne, Brian, 114
Albright, Hardie, 33, 46
Algren, Nelson, 131
Alice Adams, 47
All I Desire, 113-114
Allyson, June, 116
Alton, John, 118
Always Goodbye, 64
Ameche, Don, 70
Ammie, Come Home, 136
Anderson, Judith, 90, 104
Anderson, Michael Jr., 136
Andes, Keith, 108
Andrews, Dana, 77
Anne of Green Gables, 59
Annie Oakley, 48-49
Anybody's Girl, 29
Applause, 66
Arden, Eve, 85
Arliss, George, 29
Arms and the Girl, 47
Arnold, Edward, 70, 71
Arthur, Jean, 75
Asther, Nils, 36, 38
Autolight, 129

B.F.'s Daughter, 97-98
Baby Face, 39-41
Bacall, Lauren, 115
Back Street, 31
Ball of Fire, 73, 75-77
Banjo on My Knee, 54, 58
Bankhead, Tallulah, 108
Bara, Theda, 24
Barbara Frietchie, 18
"Barbara Stanwyck Show, The," 129, 131
Bari, Lynn, 64
Barnes, Binnie, 64, 120
Barr, Byron, 78
Barrett, Edith, 101
Barry, Gene, 126
Barrymore, John, 29
Barrymore, Lionel, 29
Bartels, Louis John, 19
Basehart, Richard, 114
Baxter, Anne, 132

Beery, Wallace, 49
Bellamy, Ralph, 31, 129
Bennett, Belle, 58
Bennett, Constance, 31
Bennett, Joan, 119
Benny, Jack, 129
Benson, Sally, 102-103
Bergman, Ingrid, 84
Bergner, Elisabeth, 88
Bettger, Lyle, 102, 113
"Beyond," 95
Beyond the Forest, 95
"Big Valley, The," 134-136
Binyon, Claude, 75
Bitter Tea of General Yen, The, 36-38
Blandick, Clara, 32
Bleeding Heart, 90
Blees, Robert, 113
Bless You, Sister, 30
Bloch, Robert, 134
Blondell, Joan, 30, 129
Blore, Eric, 64, 73
Blossoms in the Dust, 77
Blowing Wild, 115
Bochner, Lloyd, 134
Boehnel, William, 33
Bogart, Humphrey, 82, 88-89
Bogeaus, Benedict, 119
Bohnen, Roman, 66
Boles, John, 49
Bondi, Beulah, 70
Boyd, William "Stage," 21
Boyer, Charles, 79-80
Boyle, Joseph C., 19
Brackett, Charles, 76, 77, 114
Brady, Alice, 30
Brady, Scott, 121
Brand, Max, 54
Breakfast for Two, 64
Breck, Peter, 135
Breen, Richard, 115
Brennan, Walter, 54, 71
Brent, George, 33, 34, 40, 78, 85-86
Bretherton, Howard, 39
Bride Walks Out, The, 50, 64
Bride Wore Boots, The, 89-90
Bright Lights, 24, 28
Bringing Up Baby, 77
Brink, Carol Ryrie, 113
Broadway Nights, 19
Brooks, Geraldine, 93

Brown, Clarence, 105
Brown, Harry, 95
Burlesque, 19-20, 21
Busch, Niven, 104, 115
Butler, Frank, 93

Cagney, James, 17, 123-124
Cain, James, M., 82, 83, 84
Calhern, Louis, 106
California, 93, 118
Calleia, Joseph, 68
Camille, 27
Capra, Frank, 25, 26, 28, 30, 31, 36, 38, 39, 70-71, 73
Capucine, 131-132
Carleton, Marjorie, 94
Carlson, Richard, 113
Caron, Leslie, 106
Carroll, Nancy, 17, 20, 21
Carter, Ann, 89
Castle, William, 133-134
Cather, Willa, 44, 45
Catlett, Walter, 54
Cattle Queen of Montana, 118
Caulfield, Joan, 97
Chandler, Raymond, 82, 84
Chatterton, Ruth, 29, 58
Cherryman, Rex, 19, 20
Christmas in Connecticut, 87-88
City Streets, 66
Clarke, Mae, 17, 20
Clash by Night, 108, 111, 119
Cobb, Lee J., 66, 68
Coburn, Charles, 72-73, 97
Coffee, Lenore, 78
Cohn, Harry, 25, 26, 30, 31, 67
Colbert, Claudette, 70, 75
Coleman, Nancy, 78-79
Comandini, Adele, 87
Concealment, 45
Connell, Richard, 72
Connolly, Walter, 37
Conte, Richard, 95
Cook, Donald, 40
Cooper, Gary, 34, 70, 71, 73, 76-77, 115
Corey, Wendell, 102, 104-105
Cortez, Ricardo, 29, 30
Cotten, Joseph, 106
Crawford, Joan, 11, 31, 45, 102
Crime of Passion, 124-125
Cromwell, John, 54
Crowther, Bosley, 84, 131
Cry Wolf, 93-94

Cummings, Robert, 90
Cunningham, Cecil, 39

Dailey, Dan, 20
Dance of Life, The, 20
Davenport, Marcia, 103
Daves, Delmer, 84
Davis, Bette, 11, 33, 77, 84, 85, 90, 95, 102
Davis, Luther, 97
Davis, Nancy, 103
de Havilland, Olivia, 77
De Santis, Joe, 106
de Toth, Andre, 95
"Decision," 129
Decker, Marge, 105
Dehner, John, 125
DeMille, Cecil B., 65-66
DeMille, Katherine, 54
Destiny, 80
Dickson, Gloria, 81
Dieterle, William, 45
Dietrich, Marlene, 11
Dinelli, Mel, 112
Dix, Beulah Marie, 41
Dmytryk, Edward, 131
Dodd, Claire, 43, 44
Dodsworth, 58
Donaldson, Walter, 17
Donavan, Hobart, 119
Donlevy, Brian, 74
Donnelly, Ruth, 39
Double Indemnity, 13, 40, 82-84, 90, 92
Douglas, Kirk, 90-92
Douglas, Melvyn, 48
Douglas, Paul, 108, 116
Dumbrille, Douglass, 40
Duncan, Isadora, 16
Dunne, Irene, 31
Duvivier, Julien, 79
Dvorak, Ann, 39
Dwan, Allan, 118, 119

East Side, West Side, 103
Ebsen, Buddy, 54
Eburne, Maude, 39
Edelman, Lou, 130
Edwards, Ralph, 129
Egan, Richard, 136
Eisinger, Jo, 125
Eldredge, John, 45, 51
Epstein, Philip G., 64
Ericson, John, 126
Erskine, Chester, 116

Escape to Burma, 119
Evans, Linda, 135
Ever in My Heart, 41-43
Executive Suite, 116

Farmer, Frances, 66
Farrell, Glenda, 64
Farrell, Henry, 136
Farrow, John, 93
Fay, Dion Anthony, 24, 48, 111-112
Fay, Frank, 20, 21, 24, 26, 28, 35, 43, 48, 111
Feldman, Charles K., 131
Fenton, Frank, 123
Ferber, Edna, 32
File on Thelma Jordan, The (Thelma Jordan), 102
Fitzgerald, Barry, 51
Fitzgerald, Geraldine, 78
Fitzgerald and Pride, 137
Fitzmaurice, George, 21
Flesh and Fantasy, 79-80, 81
Fletcher, Lucille, 99
Florey, Robert, 45
Flynn, Errol, 93-94
Foch, Nina, 116
Fodor, Ladislas, 95
Fonda, Henry, 64, 72-73, 75, 77
Fonda, Jane, 132
Fontaine, Joan, 76, 77
Forbidden, 31
Ford, Glenn, 118, 119
Ford, John, 51-54, 65, 135
Forty Guns, 126-128
Foster, Dianne, 118
Foster, Preston, 39, 48, 51-52
Fountainhead, The, 94
Fowler, Gene, 49
Fregonese, Hugo, 115
Frings, Ketti, 102
Fuller, Samuel, 126, 128
Furies, The, 104-105

G-String Murders, The, 81
Gable, Clark, 30, 102, 105
Gallant Lady, 64
Gambling Lady, 43-44
Gardella, Kay, 129
Gardiner, Reginald, 87
Gardner, Ava, 103
Garrett, Oliver H.P., 30
Garfield, Jules (John), 66
Garson, Greer, 77
Gaslight, 84, 129

Gay Paree, 17
Gay Sisters, The, 78-79
Gilbert, Billy, 50
Gilmour, Clyde, 117
God's Gift to Women, 28
Godfrey, Peter, 87, 88, 93, 94
Golden Boy, 66-68, 116
Goldwyn, Samuel, 58, 59, 60, 62, 73, 75
Gombell, Minna, 54
Good Earth, The, 63
Goodman, Ezra, 13, 135
Gordon, Leon, 51
Gordon, Michael, 101
Grable, Betty, 20
Graves, Ralph, 27
Great Man's Lady, The, 73-75, 78
Green, Alfred E., 40
Greene, W. Howard, 118
Gregory, James, 74
Grey, Zane, 123
Gribble, Harry Wagstaff, 59
Guffey, Burnett, 118
Gunn, James, 81, 113
Guthrie, Carl, 94

Hale, Alan, 61
Hall, Mordaunt, 26
Hamilton, Harry, 54
Harburg, E.Y., 93
Harding, Ann, 20, 64
Hardy, Sam, 19, 22, 30
Harvey, Laurence, 131
Hawks, Howard, 77
Hawley, Cameron, 116
Hayden, Sterling, 124, 125
Hayes, Alfred, 108
Hayward, Susan, 137
Hayworth, Rita, 11
Head, Edith, 81, 93
Heat of Anger, 137
Heflin, Van, 90-92, 97, 103
Hepburn, Katharine, 47, 88
Her Enlisted Man, 47
High, Wide and Handsome, 66
His Brother's Wife, 51
His Girl Friday, 77
Hold Back the Dawn, 77
Holden, William, 67, 116
Holloway, Sterling, 70
Hollywood Canteen, 84-85
Hopkins, Arthur, 19
House That Wouldn't Die, The, 136
Houser, Lionel, 87

Hoyt, John, 101
Huggins, Roy, 101
Hunter, Ian, 64
Hunter, Ross, 114, 119
Huston, Walter, 104
Hyams, Joe, 130

I Married a Dead Man, 102
Illicit, 28
Informer, The, 52
Instruct My Sorrows, 85
Internes Can't Take Money, 54-55, 64
Irene, 97
Irish, William, 102
Irwin, Wallace, 45
Island of Lost Souls, The, 22
It Happened One Night, 47

James, Joni, 121
James, Rian, 55
Janney, William, 22
Jason, Leigh, 50, 64
Jaynes, Clare, 85
Jennings, Talbot, 119
Jeopardy, 112-113
Job, Thomas, 88
"Joey Bishop Show, The," 132
Johnny Belinda, 101
Johnny Guitar, 120
Johnson, Nunnally, 54

Kane, Joseph, 123
Kane, Robert, 19
Kaye, Danny, 77
Kazan, Elia, 66
Keene, Carolyn, 94
Keep Kool, 17
Keighley, William, 39
Keim, Betty Lou, 124
Keith, Brian, 118
Kenton, Erle C., 22
Kerrigan, J.M., 65
Kiam, Omar, 62
Kind Lady, 112
Knowles, Patric, 90
Kolker, Henry, 40
Korda, Alexander, 25
Kruger, Otto, 41, 42

LaHiff, Billy, 17
La Rocque, Rod, 21
Ladies of Leisure, 25, 26, 27, 28, 43
Ladies of the Evening, 25

Ladies They Talk About, 39
Lady Eve, The, 72-73, 75, 77
Lady Gambles, The, 101
Lady of Burlesque, 81
Lady of the Tropics, 66
Lahr, Bert, 20
Laine, Frankie, 115
Lamarr, Hedy, 66
Lancaster, Burt, 99
Lanfield, Sidney, 47, 64
Lang, Fritz, 108, 111
Laughton, Charles, 22
LeRoy, Mervyn, 103
Lee, Gypsy Rose, 81
Lehman, Ernest, 116
Leisen, Mitchell, 68-70, 102
Lennart, Isobel, 103
Leonard, Robert Z., 97
Letters, The, 137, 139
Levant, Oscar, 20
Lewis, David, 95
Lie, The, 102
Life and Death of John Doe, The, 70
Lightner, Winnie, 17
Lilac Time, 21
Lindsay, Earl, 16, 17
Lindsay, Margaret, 40
Lipscomb, W.P., 49
Little Foxes, The, 77
Litvak, Anatole, 99, 100
Locked Door, The, 19, 21, 24
Lombard, Carole, 20, 102
Long, Richard, 135
Longstreet, Stephen, 78
Lord, Pauline, 19
Lord, Robert, 34
"Loretta Young Show, The," 129
Lost Horizon, 37
Love Lies Bleeding, 90
Lugosi, Bela, 22
Lund, John, 102
Lupino, Ida, 137
"Lux Radio Theatre," 70, 101
Lyndon, Barré, 105
Lynn, Diana, 90

Mack, James "Buck," 14, 24, 66, 68, 111
Mack, Willard, 17, 18
MacMurray, Fred, 20, 69, 82-84, 115, 119-120
Mad Miss Manton, The, 64-65, 72
Madame X, 29
Majors, Lee, 135

Mamoulian, Rouben, 66, 67, 68
Man With a Cloak, The, 106
Mann, Anthony, 104
Manners, David, 30
Mansfield, Wanda, 17
Mantle, Burns, 43
March, Fredric, 116
Maricle, Leona, 85
Markey, Gene, 40
Marquand, J.P., 97
Marshall, Herbert, 64
Martin, Marion, 81
Martin, Tony, 54
Marvin, Lee, 129
Marx, Marian (Mrs. Zeppo), 50, 66
Marx, Zeppo, 50-51, 68
Mason, James, 103
Maté, Rudolph, 118
Matrimonial Bed, The, 24
Maverick Queen, The, 120-123
Mayo, Archie, 29, 41, 43
Mayo, Virginia, 77
McCrea, Joel, 43-44, 54, 55
McNally, Stephen, 101
McPherson, Aimee Semple, 30
Meehan, John, 51
Meeker, Ralph, 112
Meet John Doe, 70-72, 73
Menjou, Adolphe, 31, 66, 68
Merrill, Dina, 137
Merrill, Gary, 116
Message to Garcia, A, 49-50
Mexicali Rose, 22, 24, 25
Michaels, Barbara, 136
Milan, Lita, 118
Milestone, Lewis, 90
Milhauser, Bertram, 41
Milland, Ray, 93, 101
Million Dollar Legs, 67
Miracle Woman, The, 30-31, 43
Monroe, Marilyn, 108, 111, 128
Moonlighter, The, 115
Moore, Colleen, 32
Moore, Dickie, 33
Moorehead, Agnes, 99, 100
Moorhead, Natalie, 29
Morgan, Dennis, 87
Morgan, Frank, 45, 120
Mori, Toshia, 36
Moxey, John Llewellyn, 136
Mudlark, The, 34
Murrow, Edward R., 129
My Reputation, 13, 85-87, 88

Mystery Street, 112

Neal, Patricia, 94-95
Negulesco, Jean, 114
Nelson, Gene, 137
Nelson, Lori, 113
Nichols, Dudley, 52
Nielsen, Leslie, 137
Night Flower, The, 34
Night in Venice, A., 17
Night Nurse, 30, 34, 105
Night of January 16th, The, 70
Night Walker, The, 133-134
Niven, David, 95
No Man of Her Own, 102
Nolan, Lloyd, 55
Noose, The, 17, 18, 19, 25, 26
North Shore, 45
Nugent, Frank S., 70
Nugent, Judy, 119

O'Brien, Pat, 43
O'Casey, Sean, 51-52
O'Connell, Arthur, 137
O'Connor, Una, 51
O'Day, Dawn (Anne Shirley), 33, 59
O'Dea, Denis, 51
Odets, Clifford, 66, 67, 108
Odds on Mrs. Oakley, The, 89
Of Human Bondage, 54
O'Moore, Pat, 89
O'Neil, Barbara, 60, 61
Orry-Kelly, 39, 45
O'Shea, Michael, 81
Oswald, Gerd, 125
Other Love, The, 95
Owsley, Monroe, 29

Paramore, Edward, 36
Parker, Jean, 20
Parkins, Barbara, 136-137
Parrott, Ursula, 119
Patterson, Elizabeth, 70
Pearson, Humphrey, 46
Peper, William, 133
Perreau, Gigi
"Person to Person," 129
Petrie, Howard, 121
Pichel, Irving, 90
Pidgeon, Walter, 116
Plough and the Stars, The, 51-54, 65
Plunkett, Walter, 53, 106
Poe, Edgar Allan, 106

Polglase, Van Nest, 53
Polito, Sol, 100
Pollock, Channing, 21
Possessed, 31
Powell, Dick, 129
Powers, Tom 82
Pratt, Purnell, 46
Presley, Elvis, 132-133
Presnell, Robert, 72
Preston, Robert, 65, 101
Prison Farm, 67
Prouty, Olive Higgins, 58
Psycho, 134
Purcell, Gertrude, 59
Purchase Price, The, 33-35, 73
Pygmalion, 27

Queen Christina, 66
Quinn, Anthony, 115
Quo Vadis, 105

Raft, George, 83
Rainer, Luise, 63
Rand, Ayn, 70, 94
Rankin, Arthur, 22
Ransford, Maurice, 115
Rapper, Irving, 78
"Rawhide," 132
Raymond, Gene, 45, 50
Reagan, Ronald, 117, 136
Rebecca, 76
Red Salute, 46-47
Reed, Phillip, 45
Reeves, Theodore, 55
Reisch, Walter, 115
Remarque, Erich Maria, 95
Remember the Night, 68-70, 102
Rennie, James, 29
Reynolds, William, 119
Rich, Irene, 45
Ridgely, John, 85
Riskin, Robert, 70, 71
Ritt, Martin, 66
Ritter, Thelma, 114
Robinson, Earl, 93
Robinson, Edward G., 82-83
Rogue Song, The, 29
Roland, Gilbert, 105
Roland, Ruth, 39
Roman, Ruth, 115
Romero, Cesar, 64
Rose Marie, 51
Roseland, 29

Rossen, Robert, 90
Roth, Lillian, 39
Rough Company, 118
Roustabout, 132-133
Rowland, Roy, 115, 116, 124
Rozsa, Miklos, 84, 95, 125
Ruggles, Wesley, 75
Runaway Daughter, 47
Ryan, Robert, 108, 111, 119

Sakall, S.Z., 87
Sale, Chic, 17
San Francisco, 51
Sanders, George, 116
Sangster, Jimmy, 137
Santell, Alfred, 55, 64
Schenck, Joseph, 21
Schnee, Charles, 102
Schoenfeld, Bernard, 120
Scola, Kathryn, 40, 64
Scott, Lizabeth, 92
Secret Bride, The, 45
Seff, Manuel, 46
Segall, Harry, 89
Seiter, William A., 57
Seitz, John, 84
Sennwald, Andre, 46
Shanghai Express, 37
Shearer, Norma, 31, 36, 97
Shields, Arthur, 51
Shirley, Anne (Dawn O'Day), 33, 58-60
Shoemaker, Ann, 59
Shopworn, 32
Show of Shows, The, 22
Sidney, Sylvia, 19
Sign on the Door, The, 21
Silver Cord, The, 54
Siodmak, Robert, 102
Sirk, Douglas, 113
Skelly, Hal, 19, 20
Skouras, Edith, 64
Slippery Pearls, The, 36
Small, Edward, 46
Smith, Alexis, 88
Smith, C. Aubrey, 44
Snow White and the Seven Dwarfs, 76
So Big, 32-33
Somewhere I'll Find Him, 123
Son of the Sheik, The, 21
Song Is Born, A, 77
Sorry, Wrong Number, 99-101
Stage Door Canteen, 84
Stanwyck, Jane, 18

Stella Dallas, 33, 58-64
Stevens, Byron (brother), 14
Stevens, Byron (father), 14
Stevens, Catherine McGee, 14
Stevens, George, 47-48
Stevens, Mildred, 14
Stolen Life, A, 85
Stone, Grace Zaring, 36
Stopover, 113
Strange Love of Martha Ivers, The, 90-92
Strauss, Theodore, 93
Stringer, Arthur, 34
Stromberg, Hunt, 81
Sturges, John, 112-113
Sturges, Preston, 68, 72
Sullivan, Barry, 112, 121, 126
Sunset Boulevard, 13
Suspicion, 76, 77
Swanson, Gloria, 13
Swerling, Jo, 27, 29, 30, 31
Swing High, Swing Low, 20

Talbot, Lyle, 34
Tales of Manhattan, 79
Talmadge, Norma, 21
Tarkington, Booth, 47
Taste of Evil, A, 136-137
Tattle Tales, 43
Tavern, The, 17
Taylor, Robert, 50-51, 57, 66, 68, 80, 88, 97, 105-106, 111, 133-134
Ten Cents a Dance, 29-30
Thelma Jordan (File on Thelma Jordan), 102
There's Always Tomorrow, 119-120
These Wilder Years, 123-124
Thew, Harvey, 29
Thiess, Ursula, 111
This is My Affair, 57
"This is Your Life," 129
Thomas, Mary, 78
Thompson, Howard, 133
Tibbett, Lawrence, 29
Titanic, 114-115
To Please a Lady, 105
Tobin, Genevieve, 45
Toomey, Regis, 32
Torre, Marie, 129
Trial of Mary Dugan, The, 20
Trooper Hook, 125-126
Turney, Catherine, 85, 94, 102-103
Two Mrs. Carrolls, The, 88-89

Under a Texas Moon, 24

Undercurrent, 88
Union Pacific, 65-66

Vale, Martin, 88
Van Dyke, W.S., 51
Van Trees, James, 41
Variety Girl, 95,97
Vidor, King, 58, 59, 63, 94, 95
Violent Men, The, 118-119
Vogel, Virgil, 135
von Sternberg, Josef, 37

Wagner, Robert, 114
"Wagon Train," 132
Walk in the Sun, A, 90
Walk on the Wild Side, A, 130, 131-132
Walker, Joseph, 38
Wallis, Hal, 90, 104, 133
Wanger, Walter, 38
Warner, Jack, 94
Warren, Charles Marquis, 125, 126
Watson, Lucile, 85
Watters, George Manker, 19
Waxman, Franz, 88, 94, 100
Wellman, William A., 30, 33, 34, 73, 81
West, Mae, 132
Westley, Helen, 54
Webb, Clifton, 114
Wheeler, Lyle, 115
When My Baby Smiles At Me, 20
White, George, 100
White, Pearl, 14, 35
Wilder, Billy, 13, 76, 77, 82-84
Wiley, Dwight Mitchell, 90
William, Warren, 45
Wilson, Lois, 19, 120
Winn, Katherine (Kitty), 136
Winters, Shelley, 101, 116
Winterset, 55
Wise, Robert, 116
Witness to Murder, 116-117
Woman in Red, The, 45, 46
Woollcott, Alexander, 19
Wyman, Jane, 101

Yordan, Philip, 115
You Belong to Me, 73, 75
Young, Gig, 78
Young, Loretta, 129
Young, Robert, 46, 47, 50
Yurka, Blanche, 105

Ziegfeld Follies (1922), 16

ABOUT THE AUTHOR
A movie addict for many years, Jerry Vermilye is the author of books on Bette Davis and Cary Grant in the Pyramid Illustrated History of the Movies, as well as a book on Burt Lancaster. He has also written many articles for leading film magazines. A resident of Manhattan, Mr. Vermilye is movie-listings editor of *TV Guide*.

ABOUT THE EDITOR
Ted Sennett is the author of *Warner Brothers Presents*, a tribute to the great Warners films of the Thirties and Forties, and of *Lunatics and Lovers*, on the long-vanished but well-remembered "screwball" comedies of the past. He is also the editor of *The Movie Buff's Book* and has written about films for magazines and newspapers. He lives in New Jersey with his wife and three children.